Ņina Masiļūne

LATVIAN
NATIONAL
KITCHEN

Ņina Masiļūne

LATVIAN NATIONAL KITCHEN

JUMAVA

UDK 641(035)
    Ma 758

Acknownledgements:

LIDO
Hotel Konventa Sēta
Hotel Amrita
Latvijas Balzams
Latvian Country Tourism Association "Lauku ceļotājs"

Translated by *Kārlis Streips*
Edited by *Lilita Tannis*
Graphic design by *Inese Laizāne*
Photography by *Andris Tone* and *Igors Boikovs*

ISBN 9984 – 05 – 428 – 4
Printed in Latvia

CONTENTS

5

6

MEAT DISHES

VEGETABLE AND MUSHROOM DISHES

7

BREADS, PASTRY AND CAKES

SWEET SAUCES, SYRUPS AND CANDY

FOREWORD

Latvia is situated on the Baltic Sea across from Finland, Sweden and Norway. Its rich, cultural and linguistic history spans 800 years. It has always had well developed fishing and agricultural industries, and the nutrition which Latvia's residents receive has always been based primarily on livestock breeding, fishing and farming.

Since ancient times Latvians have loved rye bread, sourdough bread and wheat bread. They have used rough-ground wheat or rye flour, barley grouts and peeled barley to produce porridge. Legumes have been popular — especially gray peas with bacon. Various kinds of pancakes have been baked.

Fine-ground flour is used for various pan breads involving cottage cheese, apples and crumbs. Everyone knows the bacon-stuffed roll that is called the *pīrāgs*, and Latvians also whip up a wide variety of other baked goods — cookies, cakes and tortes. The assortment of tortes in particular is very wide.

Meat dishes come from pork, whether fresh, salted or smoked, and beef. Lamb and fowl are somewhat less common.

Fish dishes come from fish that are found on Latvia's shores, such as pilchard, cod, plaice and herring, as well as fish that are caught far away — mackerel, for example. Fresh-water fish in Latvia's waters includes carp, eel, pike, lamprey and bream.

Latvians have always been fans of cold foods, including snacks that are made from meats or fishes. Mustard and horseradish are an unfailing addition to these "cold tables". On holidays and other major events, people sit down for their meals. Many families sing Latvian folk songs or popular modern ditties after the meal is over.

Soup is often on the table in the Latvian home, and many people cannot imagine a day without freshly prepared soup. Sour cream is commonly added to Latvian soups, and there are a few which have taken on a ritual significance over the centuries. Sauerkraut soup is an example — rural weddings in Latvia are a three-day affair, and when the host brings out the sauerkraut soup, that's a sign for everybody to go home.

Among vegetables, Latvians are big potato eaters, but they also like beets, cabbage and carrots. Potatoes — boiled, baked or mashed — are an everyday food item on the Latvian menu.

Milk and dairy products are important in the Latvian cuisine, including *rūgušpiens*, *kefir*, buttermilk, cream, cottage cheese and cheese. Many Latvians prepare cheese at home. Each ethnic region has different cheese recipes, but there is one kind of cheese that is known all over the country — *Jāņu siers*, which is a cheese produced especially for the summer solstice holiday that is called *Jāņi* (although it is often available at other times of the year, too). The other key element to a summer solstice repast is beer.

11

Sauces, both warm and cold, are mostly based on sour cream.

Flavoring agents in Latvian food include onions, garlic (less commonly), parley and celery root, green onions, dill, parsley and celery parsley or dill. Caraway seeds are common, used in rye bread, sourdough bread and cheese, and added to cottage cheese, meat dishes, sauerkraut, etc.

Mushrooms or tomato purée are often added to meat dishes, soups and sauces, while wild game is usually cooked with juniper berries.

Latvia's forests burst with berries and mushrooms each year, and this is an important part of Latvian nutrition. Bilberry jam and cranberry gelatins are popular.

A typical element in Latvian housekeeping is that there is a wide range of desserts, and parties could never be imagined without them. In the Western Latvian region of Kurzeme, for example, there must be at least two desserts on the table at weddings, and one of them is always is a stewed fruit dish called *buberts*. Desserts are prepared from fruit and berries (apples, strawberries, red currants, cranberries, blackberries, etc.), rhubarb, pumpkin, carrots, cottage cheese and rye bread.

Over the centuries, field workers under the hot sun have refreshed themselves with a juice prepared from birch sap, a soured porridge called *skābputra* (in Kurzeme in particular), and various fruit and berry drinks. Beer is popular, and there are dozens of different varieties in Latvia's various regions.

ANCIENT HOUSEKEEPING.
WHAT OUR FOREBEARS ATE
DURING HOLIDAYS AND CELEBRATIONS

Ancient Latvians had four major holidays, which were associated with the positioning of the sun in the sky — the winter solstice, at Christmas, when the night is the longest, the spring and fall solstices when the day and the night are of equal length, and the summer solstice, or *Jāņi*, when the day is the longest. The winter and summer solstices have always been the major events. Each holiday has had its own typical foods, as appropriate to the time of year. Easter eggs and *Jāņi* cheese are known to have been symbols of the sun, but it can also be remembered that eggs were cooked at the spring solstice (the word for "Easter" in Latvian, "Lieldienas" as well as "Ziemassvētki" for Christmas, did not in olden days have the Christian meaning of the words, although today both Christian holidays are observed) because that is a time when hens lay lots of eggs. Cheese was made at the summer solstice because during the summer cows provide a lot of milk.

We know that foods in ancient times were often of symbolic importance. The snout of a pig, for example, may well have symbolized the plough which farmers used to till their earth. Pig's snout was cooked together with a barley sub-product called *ķūķi*, and it was thought to bring people wealth and good fortune. *Ķūķi* were made in massive mortars that were hewn from large logs. Barley would be poured into the mortar and crushed with pestles that were made especially for this purpose. The grain was thus separated from the chaff. *Ķūķi* were usually cooked shortly before the winter solstice on an evening which came to be known, logically, as *ķūķi night*. Other typical winter solstice food included peas, beans and sausages made of grouts.

A salted or dried pig's head would be boiled and then put on the table whole. The table could also hold baked pork ribs, as well as baked, dried or salted ham. Fresh ham was presented in roasts, while salted and dried ham could be cooked or baked in dough. Oven-baked potatoes and stewed sauerkraut were common side dishes. Farm families had long and ornately decorated tables, and they decorated their rooms with ornaments that could be made from straw or colored paper. These ornaments were hung from ceilings with string, so that they could wing freely.

Once the sun began to return, and spring drew near, people prepared for the next major solstice festival — Easter. Between the winter and spring solstices, however, there were other dates which the ancient Latvians never failed to note — traditional festivals on January 17, February 6 (when pig's feet and halves of pig's heads were boiled and special *pīrāgi* were baked) and March 25. On the latter date the ancients commemorated the pagan Earth goddess Māra, and special dumplings were cooked in her honor. The pagan beliefs concerning Māra's day were somewhat similar to modern-day Easter traditions.

When Easter, or the summer solstice, rolled around, eggs and cooked peas were the most typical dishes on the table. Latvians are among the many nations in the world who color their Easter eggs. Traditional Latvian eggs are green or brown, colored with birch leaves or, especially, onion skins.[1]

When the fields were covered with fine green grass, the day when the ancient deity Jurģis, or Ūsiņš, arrived. The ancients knew that this was the day when the livestock could be released to pasture for the summer, and special cheese was always produced.

The autumn solstice in olden days was usually centered around the day of Miķelis, on September 29. An animal was butchered, beer was brewed and special bread was baked. The butchering on Miķelis day most commonly involved a ram. Around Miķelis day, people stopped eating the mid-afternoon repast known as *launags*, and by Mārtiņš day, a few months later, all farm work had to be done. The grain had to be gathered and the earth had to be ploughed under, because people believed that the earth went to rest on Mārtiņš day. Shortly before that date there was also intensive work to prepare food for the winter — animals were slaughtered and prepared for keeping. On Mārtiņš day people usually ate a rooster or crested hen that was slaughtered in the deity's honor. The bird was baked and presented in clay dishes, the head and feet of the fowl intact. Accompaniments were usually stewed carrots and peas with butter. Other meat dishes on the Mārtiņš day table included grout sausages, sautéed liver and whole animal hearts. There were also baked rutabagas and carrots, oven-baked potatoes in their skins, bacon rolls, bread from rough-milled flour, and honey rolls. People added cottage cheese, butter and hemp butter to these various dishes. The Mārtiņš day cuisine also involved peas, apples and a strong and specially brewed beer to which honey was added at the last moment of brewing.

Beekeeping was a common activity in ancient Latvia, and it is very possible that many of our modern Latvian desserts are rooted in this process.

Indeed, the ancient Latvians had a very well balanced diet. They baked, they cooked, they sautéed and they fermented food in a very wide variety indeed.

---

[1] You can make beautiful onion skin-colored Easter eggs, too. Place a large quantity of onion skins in a large pot, cover with water, add a splash of vinegar, and bring to the boil. Gather a variety of small leaves and flower blossoms for decoration. Place a few of the leaves or blossoms on a raw egg and then wrap the egg in onion skins. Then wrap the egg with the skins in a layer of cheesecloth or similar cloth (discarded women's stockings work well for this purpose). Tie the ends and submerge the packet in the water. Boil for about 10 minutes. When the eggs emerge, they should be a lovely earth tone in color, with an impression of the flowers or leaves that were put on them before they were boiled. For a nice sheen, rub the eggs with a bit of raw bacon.

BEVERAGES

Beer has long since been known in Latvia. Initially the brewing of beer was a woman's work, and only later did men become involved in the process. In olden days people differentiated between "big beer", "little beer" and "warm beer". Beer was brewed with hops, without hops and with honey. When it was hot outside, people refreshed themselves with a drink that was produced by pouring hot water over rough-milled rye flour, soaking it through, adding some more hot water and then allowing the mixture to ferment. Before drinking it, people added sweet or soured milk. This drink was very similar to the modern drink called *kvass*, which is a fermented drink made from dried rye bread and its crust.

Another ancient drink was prepared by producing a dough of barley or rye malt along with some hops and then baking it in small rolls in the oven. The baked malt was then placed in a large trough that was lined with straw and then set aside to ferment.

Yet a third beverage was produced from the dregs of beer. The dregs were put into troughs along with bread crusts and then fermented. Birch sap was used to produce something similar — the sap was put into barrels, bread crusts were added, the barrels were covered with chaff and rye straw and then put in the refrigerator to sour. Eventually the rye and the chaff turned into sod, and the juice under it was sweet and sour all at once. Known as *ņirvs*, this drink was very refreshing on a hot summer day. People around the Latvian town of Kuldīga used to drink a mixture of beer and milk.

THE EVERYDAY TABLE

Every farm in ancient Latvia had a large table around which the farmer, his wife, their children and all of the farmhands gathered to eat from one big bowl until everyone was sated. Three meals a day were the rule, although from the late spring until the fall, the woman of the house also put a mid-afternoon meal on the table. Meals tended to be at fairly definite times. Breakfast in the summer was eaten around 7:00 AM — those who worked in the house took their breakfast at home, while those who were out on the fields had their breakfast brought to them there. When fields were being tilled, people took a short nap after breakfast, allowing their horses to feed. Lunch was around 11:00 AM, after which a two hour nap was common. The mid-afternoon repast was taken at 4:00 PM at the place where the person happened to be working, while supper was eaten at home, around the time when the sun was setting. If there was flax to be combed or grain to be harvested, it was often dark outside before people sat down to dinner, and then rooms were lighted with burning splinters of wood or lamps.

The table of a farm home in ancient times could never be "desecrated" with things that did not belong on it — even a hat carelessly put on the table was considered a desecration. Everyone had a specific place at the table, and on the table there were specific places for the bowl of porridge, the bowls of accompaniments and the loaf of bread. If a slice of bread fell to the floor, it was picked up, shaken off and touched to the lips, thus averting all of the evil that had become attached to the bread and making up for the carelessness of the person who dropped the bread. When the table was cleaned after meals, people carefully watched to ensure that crumbs did not fall to the floor. The ancients also believed that loud talking and laughing were inappropriate at the table, because they took away the taste of the bread. In a strictly run household, meals were quiet times. If a bite of food or a crumb accidentally fell from some-one's mouth, then someone would inevitably say, "So who is in such a big hurry?" At the end of every meal people clasped their hands and quietly said "thanks to God." Later meals were concluded with a common prayer.

LATVIAN CUISINE TODAY

The Latvian kitchen, of course, has changed beyond recognition over the last 100 years, with mo-dern conveniences such as refrigeration arriving in many households. That which is considered "tradi-tional" Latvian cuisine has not changed very much. Latvia is still very much a meat-and-potatoes society, with farm-grown vegetables playing an important role along with the catch of the Baltic Sea and the country's lakes and rivers. Sour cream is present in countless recipes. It is important for cooks in the West who use this cookbook to understand that the recipes have been prepared in recognition of the fact that not all Latvian households have access to the very latest in modern conveniences, as well as in recogni-tion of ingredients which are commonly available in Latvia. Use your cook's imagination to replace things which may not be available where you live. Several recipes, for example, call for a curdled milk dish called *rūgušpiens*. You may substitute buttermilk. Rīga Black Balsam is a very popular herb-based liqueur that is not commonly available outside of Latvia; other herb-flavored liqueurs may be used instead. Some of the dishes — head cheese, for example — may seem a bit too adventurous for you, but if you can summon up the kitchen courage to deal with a whole pig's head, then give the recipe a try, because it is delicious. A recipe with which you will not wish to experiment if you live in the United States or in some other western countries is anything that has to do with hemp. Latvians recognize the difference between hemp and marijuana, some western law enforcement agencies do not.

Similarly, do not be afraid to vary on these dishes according to your own level of experimentation and taste. The larder in Latvia has changed enormously in the last decade or so, with things that were simply not available during the Soviet occupation becoming far more readily available — many kinds of spices are the most ready examples of this. The Latvian capital city of Rīga is now home to dozens of restaurants in which the cuisine's of other lands — France, Italy, China, Thailand, Korea, Japan, Russia, Vietnam and others — are offered, and many Latvian home cooks have sought out the ingredients that are necessary to prepare foreign dishes at home. This means that if you think that some curry powder would add to any of the dishes that you find in this book, go right ahead and put some in. If it doesn't work, it doesn't work, but if it does work, you have a new version on a classic old dish. It is no accident that fusion cuisine has been all the rage in many parts of the world — people are finding imaginative ways to bring together the cooking principles of different countries and societies, and there is no reason what-soever why the Latvian cuisine could not be part of the mix.

A few words about some of the ingredients which are mentioned in this book. The word "yeast" means cake yeast. "Fat" means butter, margarine or lard, but you can also use vegetable oil if you're con-cerned about fat or cholesterol. Where a specific type of fat is needed, it is stated in the recipe. "Mustard" — use your favorite, or whichever kind seems most appropriate for the dish at hand. "Cheese" — once again, use your imagination. Almost all of the cheeses which are produced in Latvia are mild white cheeses, but some of the dishes in this book would certainly be good, if a bit different, with sharp ched-dar or the like. Do not get carried away, however — more uncommon cheeses such as Brie or Roquefort would not work. "Cottage cheese" means dry cottage cheese, which is more easily available in some parts of the world than in others. In some recipes you will see instructions to mix the cottage cheese with sour cream, and in that case you can easily substitute the creamy cottage cheese that is common in the West. When it comes to recipes for cheeses, however, dry cottage cheese is mandatory.

A note about the measurements. Latvia, like most of Europe, uses the metric system, so ingre-dients are weighed in grams and kilograms in this book. For American and other audiences, the equiva-lent in ounces and pounds is given, as well. 300 grams, for example, comes out to 10.5 ounces. Needless to say, you will not necessarily want to measure out exactly 10.5 ounces of lettuce, for example. Adjust the proportions appropriately, and you should have no problems.

One specific measurement that is used in Latvia is known as the "glass", and it is used to measure both liquids and solids. A glass is equal to 250 grams, for those of you who deal in metric measures. The American measuring unit known as the "cup" (16 tablespoons or 1/2 pint) is equal to 227 grams in fluid weight, which means that 1 glass is equal to 1.1 cups, or 1 cup plus 1 tablespoon plus a scant 2 teaspoons. In this book I have left the term "glass" in place, and assume it to mean 1 cup plus a bit more, or you can just take it to mean 1 cup and reduce the other ingredients by a bit. In those recipes where the propor-tions are important (in cakes, for example), take 1 cup, 1 tablespoon and a scant 2 teaspoons. Sometimes the life of a cook involves a bit of fuss. Sorry.

I hope that you will enjoy this cookbook, whether you have any Latvian relationships in your family or among your friends or not. Latvian cooking is good, old-fashioned and common-sense cooking which has developed over the course of many centuries, mostly in the countryside. As we say in Latvia — *labu apetīti*!

Ņina Masiļūne

Rīga, 2001

COLD DISHES
AND
APPETIZERS (SNACKS)

S A L A D S

Sauerkraut salad

300 g (10.5 oz) sauerkraut,
100 g (3.5 oz) sour cream,
5 g (0.17 oz) sugar; green onion

Squeeze as much liquid as possible from the sauerkraut, add sugar to taste, add the sour cream and mix well. Garnish with chopped green onion. If you like, you can also add some grated turnip.

Hearty potato salad with roast beef and beets

200 g (7 oz) potatoes,
100 g (3.5 oz) beets,
50 g (1.75 oz) roast beef,
50 g (1.75 oz) pickles, 2 hard-boiled eggs,
30 g (1.05 oz) medium-tart apples,
30 g (1.05 oz) herring filet,
50 g (1.75 oz) lamprey,
150 g (5.25 oz) sour cream,
salt, sugar, vinegar, mustard or horseradish

Boil the potatoes and beets in their skins, peel them, cool them and cube them. Also cube the pickles, apples, roast, herring filet and boiled eggs. Add the salt, sugar, vinegar and mustard or horseradish to taste to the sour cream and mix them with the cubed ingredients. Decorate with boiled egg, pickles and herbs. The lamprey, herring and beets can be omitted if you do not like them or if they are not easily available.

Turnip and pickle salad

100 g (3.5 oz) turnips,
100 g (3.5 oz) pickles, 40 g (1.4 oz) apple,
100 g (3.5 oz) sour cream,
salt, sugar, parsley

Wash, peel and grate turnips into slivers. Toss them thoroughly with salt and sugar to taste. Peel and dice apples. Slice and cube pickles. Mix up all of the vegetables with the sour cream and decorate with chopped parsley or a sprig of parsley placed in the center or at the edge of the bowl.

Leafy greens and cream

> 300 g (10.5 oz) lettuce,
> 40 g (1.4 oz) green onion,
> 40 g (1.4 oz) dill,
> 100 g (3.5 oz) sour cream, salt

Wash lettuce carefully, drain it and then tear it apart with your hands. Wash green onion and dill, shake off the water and chop finely with a non-rusting knife. Add dill and salt to the sour cream, pour it over the lettuce, toss, and garnish with chopped green onion.

Cucumber and radish can be added to the salad, or half of the sour cream can be replaced with curdled milk or drink called *rūgušpiens*.

Fish salad

> 300 g (10.5 oz) cooked fish filet,
> 1/2 glass peas,
> 1 hard-boiled egg,
> 1 medium-tart apple,
> 2 slices of lemon, parsley or dill,
> 1 tablespoon vinegar,
> salt, sugar, pepper

> For the dressing:
> 100 g (3.5 oz) mayonnaise,
> 1/4 glass whipped cream, 1 tablespoon of spicy tomato sauce, salt, sugar, pepper to taste

Add the flavoring agents to the mayonnaise along with the tomato sauce and the whipped cream. Cut up the fish filet, sprinkle with vinegar, salt and sugar. Set aside for 20 minutes. Chop the egg or grate it on a vegetable grater. Peel the apple and cube it. Mix all of the products carefully. Decorate with lemon slices and parsley or dill.

Cabbage, carrot and apple salad

> 200 g (7 oz) cabbage,
> 50 g (1.75 oz) carrot,
> 50 g (1.75 oz) medium-tart apples,
> 30 g (1.05 oz) horseradish,
> 100 g (3.5 oz) sour cream,
> salt, sugar, green onion

Grate the cabbage, carrots and apples, add salt and sugar to taste. Mix the sour cream with the horseradish, pour it over the vegetables and mix well. Garnish with chopped green onion.

If you do not wish to use sour cream, you may also prepare the salad just with salt, sugar and horseradish, tossing well. You can also add prunes and/or chopped nuts (if you use hazelnuts, toast them first in a pan).

Pumpkin salad

> 300 g (10.5 oz) pumpkin.

> For the syrup:
> 120 g (4.2 oz) sugar,
> 150 g (5.25 oz) vinegar,
> 150 g (5.25 oz) water, 3 cloves,
> 1 1/2 g (0.05 oz) cinnamon stick

Slice, peel and remove the seeds from the pumpkin. Use a serrated knife to cut the pumpkin into cubes. (You can use a small vegetable scoop to create pumpkin dumplings instead). Boil vinegar and water into a syrup, adding the cinnamon stick and the cloves while the syrup is cooking. Put the cubed pumpkin into the syrup and cook slowly until the pumpkin becomes transparent. Cool the pumpkin and serve with veal, fish, fowl or game.

Onion and apple salad

200 g (7 oz) onion,
100 g (3.5 oz) medium-tart apples,
2 hard-boiled eggs,
100 g (3.5 oz) sour cream,
salt, sugar, lemon juice, celery leaves

Chop up onion and rinse it four times with boiling water to which lemon juice has been added. Peel apples and cut them into slivers. Chop up the eggs. When the onions have cooled, add the sour cream and salt and sugar to taste. Stir. Decorate the salad with rings of onion that have also been rinsed in boiling water with lemon juice. Garnish with celery leaves.

Potato and herring salad

160 g (5.6 oz) potatoes,
60 g (2.1 oz) herring filet,
60 g (2.1 oz) pickles,
20 g (0.7 oz) onion,
100 g (3.5 oz) sour cream,
mustard, salt, pepper

Boil the potatoes in their skins, then peel them. Cube potatoes, pickles and herring filet and chop the onion into fine dice. Add mustard, salt and pepper to taste to the sour cream and add it to the onions, pickles and herring. Add the potatoes and toss. Decorate with cucumber slices and chopped green onion.

Potato salad can also be prepared with boiled, salted or marinated mushrooms and a mayonnaise and sour cream sauce.

Smoked Baltic pilchard salad

400 g (14 oz) smoked Baltic pilchard,
100 g (3.5 oz) fresh cucumber,
100 g (3.5 oz) sour cream, dill, salt

Peel the cucumbers. Cube the fish and the cucumbers and chop the dill fine. Mix up the sour cream with the salt and the dill and add to the fish and cucumbers. Decorate with dill.

Leek and apple salad

200 g (7 oz) leek,
200 g (7 oz) medium-tart apples,
2 hard-boiled eggs,
140 g (4.9 oz) sour cream,
salt, sugar, leek leaves

Wash the leek carefully and cut it into rounds. Slice the eggs. Peel the apples and grate them with a vegetable grater. Add the apples, along with salt and sugar to taste, to the cream. Layer the leek rounds with slices of egg in a bowl and pour the sour cream sauce over each layer. Garnish with leek leaves.

Green onion salad

150 g (5.25 oz) green onion,
20 g (0.7 oz) dill,
100 g (3.5 oz) sour cream,
salt, sugar, lemon juice

Cut up green onion and dill with a non-rusting knife. Add salt, sugar and lemon juice to the sour cream to taste, pour it over the onion and dill and mix well. Garnish with chives or dill.

19

Bean and apple salad

160 g (5.6 oz) white beans,
200 g (7 oz) medium-tart apples,
100 g (3.5 oz) sour cream,
30 g (1.05 oz) horseradish,
salt, sugar

Soak the beans overnight. Boil them until they are soft, drain and cool. Peel and grate apples on a vegetable grater. Mix together the sour cream, horseradish, salt and sugar to taste. Add in the grated apples and pour the sauce over the beans. Mix well. Garnish with parsley or dill. You can also add preserved cucumbers, boiled celery root or beets, and salted or marinated herring (a favourite Latvian delicacy).

Wild game salad

200 g (7 oz) roast wild game (moose or
   venison),
140 g (4.9 oz) marinated apples,
50 g (1.75 oz) onion,
40 g (1.4 oz) carrots,
100 g (3.5 oz) mayonnaise,
20 g (0.7 oz) tomato puree,
salt, sugar, pepper, nutmeg, parsley, marina-
   ted fruit

Slice the roast game across the grain and then sliver. Boil the carrots and sliver them and the apples. Chop the onion, blanch it with boiling water with some vinegar. Cool. Add the tomato puree and flavorings to the mayonnaise, mix together with the other ingredients, decorate with the parsley and marinated fruit.

Carrot and preserved or pickled cucumber salad

150 g (5.25 oz) carrots,
100-150 g (3.5-5.25 oz) preserved or pickled
   cucumbers,
100 g (3.5 oz) sour cream,
parsley

Boil carrots in salt water until they are almost tender. Meanwhile, peel the cucumbers. Slice carrots and cucumbers into slivers and add them to the sour cream. Garnish with parsley or carrot slices.

Salad with bacon

1 head of lettuce,
8 radishes,
50 g (1.75 oz) smoked cheese,
50 g (1.75 oz) smoked bacon,
2 tablespoons quince or lemon juice,
2 tablespoons vegetable oil,
salt, pepper, green onion

Cut up the lettuce and slice the radish. Grate the cheese. Whisk the quince juice with salt, pepper and the vegetable oil, pour the sauce over the salad and mix well. Cook the bacon, cool it and cut it up into small pieces. Toss the bacon over the salad. Garnish with chopped green onion.

Beet salad

300 g (10.5 oz) beets,
2/3 glass water,
2 g (0.07 oz) caraway seed,
20 g (0.7 oz) sugar,
50 g (1.75 oz) vinegar

Boil unpeeled beets until they are soft. Cool them, peel and slice them with a ridged knife. Put the 2/3 glass of water in a pot, add the caraway seeds, sugar and vinegar, and bring to the boil. Let cool and pour over the sliced beets. Allow beets to marinate overnight in the refrigerate. Beet salad is served with hot or cold meat dishes.

Chicken salad

200 g (7 oz) chicken,
160 g (5.6 oz) boiled potatoes,
2 hard-boiled eggs,
100 g (3.5 oz) peas,
50 g (1.75 oz) pickles,
60 g (2.1 oz) boiled carrots,
100 g (3.5 oz) mayonnaise,
10 g (.35 oz) tomato puree,
salt, sugar, vinegar, pepper, lettuce leaves

Sliver the chicken, potatoes, carrots and pickles, and finally chop the egg. Add the flavoring agents and the tomato puree to the mayonnaise. Mix together with the other ingredients. Decorate with slices of boiled egg and with the lettuce leaves.

Cucumber and sorrel salad

400 g (14 oz) cucumber,
50 g (1.75 oz) sorrel,
1/2 glass sour cream,
2 tablespoons mayonnaise,
salt, sugar, dill

Peel cucumbers and slice them into thin rounds. Toss them with salt and sugar to taste and set aside. Mix up the sour cream, mayonnaise and sorrel and pour it over the cucumbers. Garnish with dill.

Spinach can be used instead of sorrel.

Mushroom salad

300 g (10.5 oz) mushrooms,
60 g (2.1 oz) onion,
100 g (3.5 oz) sour cream,
salt, green onion

You can prepare mushroom salad with cooked, marinated or salted mushrooms. If you are using salted mushrooms, soak them in cold water to reduce the sodium content. Cut up the mushrooms into thin slivers. Chop the onions and soak them briefly in boiling water to which you have added a bit of vinegar. Combine the mushrooms and onions with the cream. Garnish with the green onions.

You can also use a vinaigrette instead of the sour cream.

Vegetable salad

100 g (3.5 oz) potatoes,
100 g (3.5 oz) preserved or pickled cucumbers,
50 g (1.75 oz) carrot,
50 g (1.75 oz) peas,
2 hard-boiled eggs,
50 g (1.75 oz) mayonnaise,
50 g (1.75 oz) sour cream,
salt, sugar, pepper, horseradish, parsley or dill

Cube boiled potatoes, cooked carrots and peeled cucumbers and chop the eggs fine. Mix up the mayonnaise and sour cream, add the flavorings to taste and mix with the other ingredients. Garnish with parsley or dill.

Spicy salad

200 g (7 oz) cooked lean beef,
200 g (7 oz) pickles,
100 g (3.5 oz) cooked carrots,
100 g (3.5 oz) pasta,
3 hard-boiled eggs,
100 g (3.5 oz) horseradish,
green onion.

For the dressing:
1 1/2 glasses sour cream,
2-3 tablespoons vinegar,
sugar, salt

Mix together all ingredients for the dressing. Add the horseradish. Boil the pasta *al dente*, drain and cool. Chop the pickles, carrots and two of the eggs. Mix all of the ingredients together. Decorate with cucumber, carrot, egg and chopped green onion. You can substitute boiled white beans for the pasta.

Celery and apple salad

300 g (10.5 oz) celery,
100 g (3.5 oz) medium-tart apples,
30 g (1.05 oz) horseradish,
100 g (3.5 oz) sour cream,
salt, sugar, celery leaves

Wash the celery and grate it fine on a vegetable grate. Peel apples and grate them into slivers. Mix up the sour cream, horseradish, salt and sugar to taste, pour the sauce over the celery and apple and mix well. Garnish with a sprig of celery leaves.

Roast beef salad

200 g (7 oz) roast beef,
100 g (3.5 oz) boiled potatoes,
100 g (3.5 oz) pickles,
2 hard-boiled eggs,
salt, sugar, pepper, mustard or horseradish,
100 g (3.5 oz) mayonnaise,
100 g (3.5 oz) sour cream,
green onion

Slice beef, potatoes, pickles and one of the eggs into slivers. Mix together mayonnaise, sour cream and spices. Add to the other ingredients. Decorate with slices of the second egg, cucumber and green onions. You may add peas if you like.

22

Stuffed tomatoes

4-5 ripe medium tomatoes

Wash the tomatoes and cut off their tops with a sharp knife. Scoop out the tomatoes with a teaspoon. Turn the tomatoes over to let the liquid drain out. Mound stuffing (see below) into them, put on the tops and arrange on a plate. You may dot sour cream over the tomatoes if you like.

1. Ham and egg stuffing

100 g (3.5 oz) ham,
1-2 hard-boiled eggs,
3 tablespoons cooked rice,
1 tablespoon chopped dill,
75 g (2.625 oz) sour cream, salt

Cube the ham and chop the eggs fine. Mix together with the sour cream, salt and dill.

2. Green (preserved) pea stuffing

Sprinkle the tomatoes with salt and pepper and put the peas into the tomatoes. You may add sour cream if you like.

3. Herring and cottage cheese stuffing

The filet of 1 whole herring,
1 medium-tart apple,
160 g (5.6 oz) dry cottage cheese,
4 tablespoons sour cream

Chop the herring filets fine, grate the peeled apple, press the cottage cheese through a sieve and mix it with the sour cream. Mix together all of the ingredients.

Beef tongue and mushroom salad

200 g (7 oz) boiled beef tongue,
100 g (3.5 oz) marinated mushrooms,
100 g (3.5 oz) boiled celery,
salt, black pepper,
100 g (3.5 oz) mayonnaise,
100 g (3.5 oz) sour cream,
parsley or dill

Sliver the tongue, celery and mushrooms. Add cream, salt and pepper to the mayonnaise and mix together with the other ingredients. Decorate with parsley, dill or mushrooms.

Chopped herring

150 g (5.25 oz) herring filet,
100 g (3.5 oz) medium-tart apples,
50 g (1.75 oz) onion,
2 hard-boiled eggs,
1/2 glass sour cream,
green onion

Peel the apples and dice them and the herring. Chop the onion and blanch it with boiling water with some vinegar. Let the onion cool. Chop one whole egg and only the white of the other egg. Mix the sour cream with the other ingredients and place in an oval dish. Decorate with finely chopped egg yolk and chopped green onion.

Stuffed cucumbers

2 preserved or pickled cucumbers,
lettuce leaves

For the filling:
100 g (3.5 oz) smoked herring filet,
20 g (0.7 oz) boiled carrot,
40 g (1.4 oz) peas,
1 hard-boiled egg,
100 g (3.5 oz) sour cream

Cut off the ends of the cucumbers, halve them and scoop out the seeds. Stuff the cucumbers with the stuffing and decorate with radish and green onion. Serve on lettuce leaves. For the stuffing, cube the herring and carrot, chop the egg fine and mix together with the sour cream.

Tomatoes in cream

300 g (10.5 oz) tomatoes,
100 g (3.5 oz) sour cream,
40 g (1.4 oz) green or white onion, salt

Wash the tomatoes and cut them into rounds or slices with a sharp, non-rusting knife. Arrange them on a plate, sprinkle with salt. Pour the sour cream over the tomatoes and then scatter chopped green onion or lightly blanched white onion rings across them.

You can also pour your favorite vinaigrette over the tomatoes, mixing up equal amounts of oil and vinegar (40 g (1.4 oz) in all), adding salt, white pepper and sugar. Cucumbers can be prepared in this same way, too.

Soaked bilberry and apple salad

1 kg (2 lb, 3 oz) bilberries,
0.5 kg medium-tart apple,
1 l (1 quart + 4 tablespoons) water,
300 g (10.5 oz) sugar

Blanch the bilberries in water and arrange them in layers in a glass jar with slivered peeled apple. Boil the water with the sugar and pour it over the berries and apples. Seal the jar properly and store in the refrigerator. The salad can be served with meat, fowl and wild game.

Tomato and egg salad

200 g (7 oz) tomatoes, salt, parsley or dill
2 hard-boiled eggs, 100 g (3.5 oz) sour cream,

Wash and dry some medium-sized tomatoes and cut them into slices with a sharp, non-rusting knife. Quarter the hard-boiled eggs lengthwise. Add salt to the sour cream. Layer the tomato slices and eggs in a bowl, pouring some sour cream over each layer. Decorate the salad with extra slices of tomato and sprigs of parsley.

Fresh cucumber in cream

200 g (7 oz) cucumber,
100 g (3.5 oz) sour cream, salt, dill, green onion

Wash and peel the cucumbers (non-waxed cucumbers can be left unpeeled), slice and cover them with sour cream, to which first add the salt. Sprinkle chopped dill and green onion over cucumbers. Garnish with circles of cucumber.

FISH DISHES

Horseradish cream

1 glass heavy cream,
2 tablespoons horseradish,
salt, sugar

Whip the cream to stiff peaks and add the horseradish and salt and sugar to taste. If you wish to maintain a stiff consistency to the cream, first add 1 teaspoon of dissolved gelatin to the horseradish and only then mix it with the whipped cream.

Marinated onions

300 g (10.5 oz) onion,
200 g (7 oz) vinegar,
100 g (3.5 oz) water,
40 g (1.4 oz) sugar,
salt, white pepper, black pepper, bay leaves

Peel and wash the onions. Cut them into rings. Boil water adding vinegar, sugar, salt, pepper and bay leaves. Put the onions in a jar and pour the vinegar water over them to cover. Cover the jar. When the marinade has cooled, arrange the onions in a dish and pour some of the marinade over them. Marinated onions can be used to accompany various fish dishes.

Fish in carrot and tomato sauce

300 g (10.5 oz) fresh fish filet (cod,
pike or perch),
1 tablespoon flour,
salt,
vegetable oil for frying

For the sauce:
2 carrots,
1 onion,
1 small bunch parsley,
1 small piece celery root,
30 g (1.05 oz) vegetable oil,
100 g (3.5 oz) spicy tomato sauce,
1/2 teaspoon potato starch,
water

Slice the fish filets and roll them in the flour. Pan-fry until ready. Arrange the slices on a plate and pour the hot sauce over them. Serve cooled. Decorate with marinated onions and parsley.

For the sauce: grate the carrot, the onion, the parsley and the celery and sauté for 5 minutes. Add the spicy tomato sauce. Mix well. Add the potato starch, stir, add a bit of water and bring to a boil. If you want the sauce to be more flavorful, add pepper, bay leaves, vinegar, sugar and salt to taste.

Lightly salted salmon

1 kg (2 lb, 3 oz) fresh salmon filets,
2–3 tablespoons salt,
1/2–1 tablespoon sugar,
black pepper;
150 g (5.25 oz) onion

Clean and filet a salmon, or buy four fresh salmon filets. Pat the filets dry with a clean towel. Mix together 3 parts salt and 1 part sugar and pour over a kitchen board. Dredge the salmon through the salt and sugar to cover. Put the filets, skin side up, in a dish, weight them down, cover them and put them in the refrigerator for 6-12 hours. When ready to serve, slice the filets diagonally and arrange on a plate. You may roll some of the filets and fasten them with toothpicks if necessary. Sprinkle black pepper over the filets. Decorate with rings of marinated onions with dill or parsley sprigs. You may also use sliced lemon. The same recipe can be used for trout filets, but then the proportions of the salt and sugar should be 1:1 or 2:1, as you like.

Saukas

250 cooked pork (it may be fatty),
150 g (5.25 oz) salted herring filet,
1/3 glass sour cream,
green onion

Dice the pork, lightly brow in a pan. When the pork has cooked mix it with the herring filets. Arrange on a plate and pour the sour cream over it. Sprinkle generously with chopped green onion.

Lightly salted cod filet

1 kg (2 lb,
3 oz) cod filet,
2-3 tablespoons salt,
1 teaspoon spices (white and black pepper,
coriander, nutmeg and cloves, ground and
combined to measure 1 teaspoon), 1-2 table-
spoons of Rīga Black Balsam (a specialty
liqueur available in Latvia and in major
Latvian centers in the West) or another
dark herb-based liquer

Sprinkle the salt and the spices over the cod filets and weight them down. Set aside for 6 hours. Sprinkle with the liqueur, re-weight and set aside for four hours. Slice before serving.

Caviar

400 g (14 oz) salmon roe,
20 g (0.7 oz) salt

Pour boiling water over the roe and stir until the outer shell of the roe separates. Put the roe into a sieve and drain thoroughly. Place in a glass jar, sprinkle with salt and mix well. Set aside in the refrigerator for 8 hours. You may also add pepper and 2 tablespoons of vegetable or olive oil if you like. The roe is most often used as a flavoring for sandwiches.

Fish in aspic

1 kg (2 lb, 3 oz) fresh fish (carp, eel, perch),
1 l (1 quart + 4 tablespoons) water,
50 g (1.75 oz) flavoring vegetables,
pepper, bay leaves, salt,
20 g (0.7 oz) gelatin, lemon,
parsley,
1 carrot,
1 egg white

Clean and dress the fish to obtain filets. Put the fish heads, bones and tails in a pot, cover them with cold water and bring to the boil. Remove any foam. Add the flavoring vegetables (chopped up), the salt, pepper and bay leaves and simmer on a low flame for 30 minutes. Strain the liquid and put the fish filets in it. Simmer for another 20 minutes. Remove the fish from the liquid with a slotted spoon. Strain the liquid and add gelatin, first dissolving the gelatin in water. Add egg white , lightly beaten (this will make the liquid clearer). Heat the liquid to almost boiling, remove it from the flame and set aside for 30 minutes. Strain it again. Next boil the carrot and slice it into thin rounds. If you have a star-shaped cookie press, cut the rounds into stars, or cut them into stars with a knife. Take as many small bowls as you will need for the liquid. Place some parsley in each bowl, followed by one of the carrot stars. Add a bit of the fish liquid and allow it to set. Arrange pieces of the fish on top of the set liquid and then add more liquid to fill the bowls nearly to the top. Place the bowls in the refrigerator to allow them to set. Before serving, remove the aspic from the bowls and arrange on plates with slices of lemon. The aspic is traditionally served with horseradish — store-bought or homemade.

Pan-baked lamprey

If you get live lamprey, put them in a plastic bag and weight them lightly. When you are ready to prepare them, sprinkle the lamprey with salt and wipe them lightly with a clean cloth. Heat a heavy pan (without any fat), place the lamprey on the pan close together, bake them for 5-8 minutes, turn and bake for 4-5 minutes more. The lamprey are ready when they break if you bend them a bit. Do not overbake or let them burn, because then they will be better. If you want the lamprey to be thinner, tenderize them with a wooden meat mallet before baking. Arrange the lamprey tightly in a dish, sprinkling salt between them. Take some very strong tea or coffee, mix it with some water and pour it over the lamprey for color. Weight down the lamprey and refrigerate. Meanwhile, make an aspic (with the liquid from the lamprey dish) and use it to decorate the lamprey. You can also decorate them with lemon slices.

Homemade horseradish

200 g (7 oz) horseradish root,
80 g (2.8 oz) vinegar,
120 g (4.2 oz) water,
20 g (0.7 oz) salt,
20-40 g (0.7-1.4 oz) sugar (to taste)

Soak the horseradish root in cold water for a while, wash it, rinse it and grate it finely (or buzz it in a food processor until it forms a paste). Put the grated horseradish in a pot and cover it with boiling water. Cover the pot and let the horseradish cool. Strain the horseradish and add the vinegar, salt and sugar. Mix thoroughly. Place the horseradish in small jars, cover tightly and store in the refrigerator. The horseradish can be served with meat and fish dishes or used in various salads.

Stuffed pike (cod, perch)

1 kg (2 lb, 3 oz) pike or other fish,
75 g (2.625 oz) white bread, 2 eggs,
50 g (1.75 oz) butter,
100 g (3.5 oz) onion,
70 g (2.45 oz) heavy cream,
salt, pepper, nutmeg,
50 g (1.75 oz) flavoring vegetables

For decorations:
lemon, leek leaves, carrots, peas

Clean and dress the fish, carefully removing its skin so that it remains in one piece. Remove all of the bones from the meat of the fish and run the meat through a grinder or a food processor. Remove the crusts from the white bread and soak in milk until saturated. Chop the onions and sauté them in the butter, until translucent to brown. Add the saturated bread and the onions to the fish and reprocess. Add the eggs, salt, pepper, nutmeg and heavy cream, mix well. Carefully stuff the fish back into its skin, not packing it too tightly. Place the stuffed fish in a large soup pot and pour warm water over it to cover. Add chopped carrots, onions, parsley, celery, pepper, bay leaves and salt to taste. Place the pot on a low flame but do not cover it. Simmer the fish very slowly for approximately 90 minutes, adding more water as needed. If you have any remaining stuffing, roll it into small dumplings and cook it along with the fish. Generally speaking, the longer and more slowly the fish cooks, the tastier it will be. When the fish is cooked, carefully remove it from the pot and let it cool thoroughly. Place the fish on an oval plate and slice it, keeping the slices together so that it still looks like a whole fish. Place thin slices of lemon between the slices of fish and pile mounds of diced carrots, peas and the fish dumplings (if you cooked any) around the fish. Strain the liquid in which the fish cooked and add gelatin — 8 g of gelatin per glass of stock. When the liquid thickens, pour it carefully over the fish and the vegetables. The traditional presentation of this fish includes a leek leaf which you have covered in the thickened liquid and laid across the fish. Serve the fish with horseradish. You may also pipe decorations on the fish with horseradish cream.

Pilchard in white marinade

300 g (10.5 oz) fresh pilchard,
1 tablespoon flour,
40 g (1.4 oz) vegetable oil,
salt

For the marinade:
100 g (3.5 oz) water,
1 onion,
1 carrot,
100 g (3.5 oz) vinegar,
1/2 teaspoon sugar,
8 black peppercorns,
8 white peppercorns,
2 bay leaves

Clean the pilchards, salt them lightly and roll them in flour. Fry in heated vegetable oil until ready. Cool the fish, place it in a dish and pour the marinade over it. Marinade the fish for 2-4 hours.

For the marinade: clean and slice carrots and onions. Boil water, vinegar and spices. Cook the onion pieces lightly in this mixture. Boil carrot separately in salt water. When cooked, add the onions and carrots to the marinade.

Marinated herring rolls

2 salted herring,
1 onion,
4 cloves,
mustard seed

For the marinade:
200 g (7 oz) water,
250 g (8.75 oz) vinegar,
2 onions,
pepper, bay leaves, sugar

If the herring is very salty, first soak it in water. Clean the soaked fish and remove the filets. Sprinkle the inside of each filet with mustard seeds and cover with sliced onion. Roll up the filets, starting from the tail end, and fasten with a clove. Place the rolled herring in a glass jar, pour over the cold marinade, fasten lid and leave standing until the next day. Serve the herring and onions in a deep dish, and pour some marinade on top.

For the marinade: peel the onions, cut them into rings, place in hot water. Add pepper to taste, bay leaves, a pinch of salt and some sugar and bring to a boil. Cook until the onions become translucent. Add vinegar. Mix well and cool.

You can also cut the herring into small pieces before marinating, and the marinade can also include sunflower oil and caraway seeds. Substitute horseradish for the mustard seeds for a different taste.

Salt pilchard can be prepared in the same way.

Fish loaves with cheese

1 kg (2 lb, 3 oz) cod filet,
5 g (0.175 oz) white bread,
100 g (3.5 oz) bacon,
2 eggs,
2 tablespoons butter,
100 g (3.5 oz) onion,
2 tablespoons sweet cream,
pepper, salt,
3 carrots,
100 g (3.5 oz) mild cheese

Remove the skin from the cod filets and put them and the bacon through a grinder or a food processor. Sauté the chopped onion in butter and add it and white bread which you have soaked in water to saturation to the fish. Add the eggs, salt, spices and cream and mix thoroughly. Slice the carrots into thin rounds and arrange them in a loaf pan. With damp hands, shape the fish into two loaves and put them on top of the carrots. Brush melted butter over the fish loaves and add water up to about one-half of the height of the loaves. Bake in the oven for 1 hour. During the baking, add salt and bay leaves to the water. Five minutes before the fish is ready, grate the cheese and sprinkle it across the loaves. Allow the loaves to cool, cut them into slices and decorate them with radishes, cucumber and lettuce leaves.

Fish gelatin

> 600 g (21 oz) fish heads and bones,
> 1 slice carrot,
> 1/2 onion,
> parsley,
> celery,
> 6 peppercorns,
> 1 bay leaf, salt,
> 1 tablespoon quince or lemon juice,
> 25 g (0.875 oz) gelatin

Remove the gills from the fish heads. Wash the fish heads and bones. Place them in a pot and add cold water to cover. Add the quince or lemon juice. Bring the liquid to a boil, remove any foam, and add the flavoring vegetables and spices. Put the pot on a low flame and simmer for 1 hour. Strain the liquid and add the gelatin (which you have first dissolved in water). When the gelatin has dissolved thoroughly, strain the liquid through two layers of damp cheesecloth. After the gelatin has been added, you may also add 1-2 beaten egg whites. Mix thoroughly, heat again and set aside for 30 minutes before straining again (this makes the liquid clearer).

Put 1 tablespoon of fish gelatin into some cold water to saturate, then put the dish into a hot water bath to dissolve the gelatin. When the gelatin is dissolved, mix it with 1 cup horseradish cream.

Fish dumplings in aspic

> 500 g (17.5 oz) fish filet (perch, pike, etc.),
> 1 slice white bread,
> 2 eggs,

> 1 onion,
> 50 g (1.75 oz) butter,
> 100 g (3.5 oz) sweet cream,
> salt, pepper, nutmeg,
> 600 g (21 oz) fish gelatin (see below)

For decoration:
> 1 hard-boiled egg white,
> 1 boiled carrot, parsley,
> 120 g (4.2 oz) horseradish cream or mayonnaise gelatin

Remove the skin from the fish filets and run them through a grinder or food processor twice. Before the second grinding, chop up the onion and sauté it in some butter until it is translucent. Soak the bread in water until saturated. Add the onions and the bread (you may substitute 3 tablespoons of manna-croup for the bread) to the fish and grind it for the second time. Add the eggs, pepper, salt and nutmeg, stirring all the while. Gradually pour in the cream. Mix the mass thoroughly. With damp hands, form small dumplings of fish. Sauté them in some fish stock until cooked through and set aside to cool.

Rinse some wine glasses with cold water and pour some slightly set fish gelatin into each one. On top of the gelatin, arrange decoratively cut carrot slices, some of the egg white and a leaf of parsley. Allow the gelatin to set thoroughly. Next put 1 cm (0.4 inch) of horseradish cream or mayonnaise gelatin in each glass. When it has hardened, place four or five fish dumplings in each glass. Pour in the fish gelatin to cover and allow the gelatin to set thoroughly. Before serving, remove the gelatin from the glasses and decorate it with lettuce leaves.

Fish in sour cream sauce

400 g (14 oz) fresh fish filet (cod, perch or the like),
salt, flour, vegetable oil

For the sauce:
1 glass sour cream,
1 teaspoon butter,
1/2 teaspoon mustard or 1 teaspoon horseradish,
salt,
2 hard-boiled eggs

Slice the filet and salt it. Roll it in flour and pan-fry until ready. Cool the fish, arrange it on an oval plate, pour the sauce over it and sprinkle a chopped boiled egg over the dish. Decorate with sliced cucumber and parsley.

For the sauce: melt the butter in a pan, add the mustard or horseradish, sour cream, salt and two finely chopped hard-boiled eggs. Heat, stirring all the while. Do not boil.

Marinated mackerel

1 kg (2 lb, 3 oz) mackerel,
2 onions,
mustard,
1 1/2 glasses marinade,
1/2 teaspoon cinnamon,
2 teaspoons vegetable oil

For the marinade:
1 glass vinegar,
3/4 glasses water,
6 peppercorns,
1-2 cloves,
1 bay leaf,
1 chopped onion,
1 teaspoon sugar, salt

First make the marinade: Put all of the ingredients except the vinegar in a pot and bring to a boil. Add the vinegar and strain.

Clean and dress the mackerel to obtain filets. Cover the filets with a thin layer of mustard and cut them into bite-sized pieces. Cut the onions into thin rings. Put the fish and onions in a deep dish and cover them with cold marinade and the vegetable oil. Sprinkle the cinnamon over the fish and cover the dish. Allow the fish to marinate for 12 hours before serving. Serves 10.

Fish in mayonnaise sauce

400 g (14 oz) fresh fish filet (cod or pike),
flour,
vegetable oil,
1 teaspoon lemon juice,
salt

For the sauce:
100 g (3.5 oz) mayonnaise,
1 teaspoon lemon juice,
1-2 teaspoons spicy tomato sauce,
1 teaspoon sugar,
3 tablespoons whipped cream.

Mix together all of the ingredients for the sauce. Slice the filets and sprinkle the lemon juice over them. Set aside for 20 minutes. Roll the filets in flour and fry in hot oil until ready. Let the fish cool. Arrange it on a plate and pour the sauce over it. Decorate with lemon slices. If you wish to use salmon or other fattier fish, cook it first in vegetable stock.

Smoked pilchard in aspic

600-800 g (21-28 oz) smoked pilchard filets,
1 1/2 glasses water,
1/2 glass vinegar,
6 peppercorns,
2 bay leaves,
2 onions,
salt, sugar,
1 tablespoon gelatin

Remove the skin from the filets. Slice the fish and place in small bowls. Cover with chopped onion and strained marinade (see below) to cover. Allow to set. Remove the aspic from the bowls before serving and decorate with lettuce leaves. For the marinade: put the water, spices, salt and sugar in a pot and bring to the boil. Add the vinegar and gelatin, which you have first put in cold water to saturate. When the gelatin has dissolved, strain the marinade.

COLD DISHES AND APPETIZERS (SNACKS)

Bean and apple salad

Sauerkraut salad

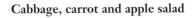

Cabbage, carrot and apple salad

Mushroom salad

COLD DISHES AND APPETIZERS

Cold fish dish

Marinated herring rolls

COLD DISHES AND APPETIZERS (SNACKS)

Stuffed fish, smoked pilchard

Pan-baked lamprey

Delicious food and refreshing drinks...

Jāņa sēta

❀ ... makes our life brighter. For a moment forget your duties and hurry.
Enjoy the great atmosphere of the summer beer garden, delicious food as well as excellent service. Come alone, come with your colleagues and partners, come with your family and friends!

❀ **Summer terrace "JANA SETA" is waiting for you every day from 12:00 until 23:00**
Call for reservation: 7087580

Hotel Konventa Sēta ★★★

9/11, Kalēju Str.

MEAT DISHES

Head cheese

1 pig's head,
100 g (3.5 oz) vegetables,
pepper, bay leaves, salt forflavour

Cut the pig head open from the bottom without cutting all the way through. Remove the brains of the pig head. Wash the head thoroughly and place it, along with the tongue of the pig, in a pot of boiling water. Bring to a boil, remove any foam, and add onions, carrots, celery and spices for flavour. Boil until the meat is tender enough to remove from the bone. Remove the pig's head from the liquid and remove the skin and 1/2 centimeter of the fat, keeping it in one piece. Dice the rest of the meat, the ears and the tongue. Moisten a cloth napkin or several layers of cheesecloth. Place the skin on the napkin, fat side up. Mound the meat on the skin, sprinkle with salt and pepper then fold up the edges of the skin. Bring the corners of the napkin or cheesecloth together and tie them tightly with a string. Place the bundle back into the cooking liquid and simmer for 30 minutes. Remove the bundle from the liquid, allow it to cool slightly and weight it down. Remove the weight after 6-8 hours and unwrap the meat. Slice the meat and arrange it on a plate. Decorate with pickle rounds and parsley or dill.

Stuffed pig's head

1 pig's head (approximately 1.2 kg (42 oz)),
300 g (10.5 oz) pork,
150 g (5.25 oz) beef tongue,
2 eggs,
100 g (3.5 oz) sweet cream,
100 g (3.5 oz) flavoring vegetables (onion,
  parsley, celery, carrots),
pepper, bay leaves, salt, sugar,
1 g (0.035) chemically pure nitrate

Wash the pig's head and blanch it in boiling water. Remove the skin, taking care to keep it in one piece with the bones. Cut up the meat, add the salt, sugar and nitrate, place it in a bowl, cover it, and refrigerate it for 24 hours. Sew up the eyes and snout of the skin and put it into salt water to soak.

After 24 hours, grind the meat several times. Dice the beef tongue and add it to the meat with eggs and cream. Stuff the meat into the skin of the pig's head. Wrap it in a napkin or cheesecloth, tie up the bundle, and put it in a pot. Pour in hot water to cover, add the flavoring vegetables, spices and salt and boil until done. Remove from the liquid and let the bundle cool. Unwrap it. To serve, cut the meat into slices, arrange them in a bowl and decorate with peas, pickles and parsley or dill.

33

Stuffed chicken

1 chicken (1-1 1/2 kg (2 1/2-3 1/2 lb)),
150 g (5.25 oz) pork, 1-2 eggs,
2 slices white bread without the crusts and
  soaked in milk,
3/4 glass milk,
2 tablespoons butter,
salt, pepper, nutmeg

Dress and wash the chicken. Cut open the skin above the backbone and remove the skin carefully from the body of the chicken. Remove all of the meat from the chicken and grind in food processor, reserving one large filet. Grind pork with chicken two times. Add the milk bread. Process again. Melt butter and add the eggs, salt, pepper, a pinch of nutmeg and milk. Mix the mass thoroughly. Sew together the chicken skin, leaving an opening at the neck for stuffing. Cut the chicken filet lengthwise and place the slices in the middle of the mass of meat. Stuff the meat loosely into the skin and sew up the chicken. If there is more meat, you can cook it into dumplings.

Place some sliced carrot and parsley in a loaf pan. Put the stuffed chicken skin on top of the carrot and parsley. Make some bouillon with the chicken bones and pour some of it into the pan. Bake the chicken in a medium oven for 60-90 minutes, occasionally moistening it with the bouillon. Let the chicken cool. Remove the string and slice the chicken. Decorate with baked apples stuffed with boysenberry jam (remove the tops of the apples and scoop them out; fill the apples with jam, arrange them on a pan, add a bit of water and bake in the oven, taking care to remove the apples before they fall apart; you may also stuff the apples with cranberry jam or pitted prunes).

Rolled veal

1 kg (2 lb, 3 oz) veal with ribs intact,
50 g (1.75 oz) butter,
50 g (1.75 oz) carrots,
3-4 eggs,
salt, pepper,
25 g (0.875 oz) sour cream,
water

Remove the ribs from the veal. You should have 1 kg (2 lb, 3 oz) of veal when deboned. Wash the meat, tenderize it thoroughly with a meat mallet. Rub with salt and pepper, roll tightly and let stand in the refrigerator for 30 minutes. Unroll the meat, brush butter across it, and arrange whole or sliced hard-boiled eggs and cubed carrot on top. Roll the meat tightly again, tie the ends with white thread that you have blanched in boiling water, and tie the rest of the roll with string. Place the roll in a pan, add a bit of boiling water and bake in the oven, moistening with the cooking water from time to time. During the baking, brush sour cream on the roll several times and turn it occasionally. When the meat is nearly ready, sprinkle it with salt. When the meat is ready, cool slightly and place in the refrigerator under a weight for 6 hours. Remove the weight and untie the roll. Slice the roll and arrange the slices on a shallow plate. Make some gelatin with the liquid that remains in the pan after the meat is ready. Slice it and use it to decorate the veal.

Rolled stuffed piglet

1 kg (2 lb, 3 oz) piglet meat,
50 g (1.75 oz) flavoring vegetables (carrot,
  parsley, celery),
spices

For the stuffing:
200 g (7 oz) veal,
50 g (1.75 oz) white bread soaked in water to
  saturate,
30 g (1.05 oz) sour cream,
3 eggs,
1 pork tongue,
2 pork kidneys,
salt, pepper,
water

Remove the skin from the meat, leaving approximately 1/2 cm of fat. Rub the skin and fat with salt and pepper. Grind the remaining piglet meat with the veal twice. On the second grind, add the soaked bread. Add the cream, the yolk of one of the eggs, salt, pepper and water and knead the ingredients thoroughly. Put the pig's tongue and kidneys (first slicing the kidneys in half lengthwise and soaking them in some water with vinegar) in a pot. Boil until soft. Remove the skin from the tongue and cut it into slices. Hard boil two of the eggs, peel them and cut them in half. Dampen a cloth napkin or some cheesecloth. Put the piglet skin on the napkin, skin side down. Brush beaten egg white across it and then arrange the ground meat atop the skin at a thickness of 1/2-1 cm (0.2-0.4 inch). Arrange the sliced tongue, kidneys and egg halves on top. Roll the skin with the filling into a tight roll, wrap it in the napkin and tie firmly.

Place the bundle in a pot and add boiling water to cover. Add the flavoring vegetables, salt, pepper and bay leaves and simmer on a low flame for 2-3 hours. Remove the bundle from the liquid, allow it to cool a bit and weight it down in the refrigerator for 8 hours. Remove the weight, untie the string and open up the bundle. Slice the roll, arrange it on a plate and decorate with celery parsley or dill. Serve with fresh vegetable salad and horseradish.

Rolled pork with bacon

1 kg (2 lb, 3 oz) lean pork,
200 g (7 oz) smoked bacon,
1 egg,
salt, pepper,
100 g (3.5 oz) carrots

Slice the pork 2 cm (0.8 inch) thick lengthwise. Tenderize one side of the slices with a meat hammer and rub them thoroughly with salt and pepper. Roll up the slices, wrap them in baking paper and refrigerate for three hours.

Cut the smoked bacon into thin slices. Unwrap the meat slices, brush them with the beaten egg. Place the sliced bacon on top of the meat and roll it back up into a tight roll. Tie with string. Place sliced carrots in a large casserole dish and lay the rolled pork on top of it. Pour a little hot water over the meat, add salt. Bake in the oven until ready, moistening every 10 minutes with the cooking water. When done, allow the meat to cool somewhat and weight it down lightly. Before serving, slice the meat, place it on a shallow plate and decorate with vegetables, parsley or dill.

Pork in aspic

1 kg (2 lb, 3 oz) pork,
50 g (1.75 oz) flavoring vegetables (onion,
   carrot, parsley, celery),
pepper,
bay leaves,
salt

Choose pork from a young and moderately fatty piglet for this dish (the head, knuckles and a piece of the shoulder or side). Chop the head in half and remove the brains. Wash the head. Chop the knuckles in half and cut up the rest of the meat in small pieces. Wash all of the meat. Put the meat in a pot and cover with water. Cover the pot and bring to a boil. Remove any foam. Add the vegetables and salt and simmer uncovered over a low flame. Add the pepper and bay leaves toward the end of the cooking. When the meat separates easily from the knuckles, set aside.

Remove the meat from the liquid, take it off the bone and dice. Strain the liquid and put it in the refrigerator until the fat rises to the top. Remove the fat. Prepare enough small bowls to handle all of the meat, rinsing each bowl in cold water. If you like the taste of garlic in your aspic, put some chopped garlic in each bowl first. Arrange decoratively cut pieces of boiled carrot and some parsley leaves in each bowl. Top them with the meat and cover completely with the strained bouillon. Place the bowls in the refrigerator to set. Remove the aspic from the bowls before serving. Serve with vinegar, mustard or horseradish.

Veal in aspic

1 kg (2 lb, 3 oz) veal meat and legs,
50 g (1.75 oz) flavoring vegetables (onion,
   carrot, parsley, celery),
pepper, bay leaves, salt

For this dish, choose the lesser cuts of veal (the head, the legs etc.). Dress the head and chop it in half. Remove the brains. Dress the legs and chop them up. Cut up other cuts of meat, too. Wash the meat and put it in a pot. Cover with cold water and bring to the boil. Remove any foam. Add the flavoring vegetables and salt. Bring to a boil again and add the pepper and bay leaves. Simmer on a low flame until the meat falls from the bone. Remove the meat from the liquid and take it off the bone. Grind the meat. Strain the cooking liquid. Mix the ground meat back into the cooking liquid and bring to the boil again. Rinse a large bowl with cold water and place the meat and liquid into the bowl. Refrigerate it until it sets. Before serving, remove the aspic from the bowl and slice it. Decorate with boiled and decoratively cut vegetables and parsley or dill. Serve with vinegar, mustard or horseradish.

Rolled chicken

1 chicken (1-1.5 kg (2 1/2-3 1/2 lb)),
salt,
butter,
2-3 garlic cloves,
pepper

Choose a young, meaty chicken for this dish. Dress the chicken, removing its neck and wings. Cut open the skin above the backbone and, starting from the back, remove the skin and the meat from the bone. Make a bouillon from the wings, neck and bones. Place the chicken meat, skin side down, on a board, sprinkle with salt, brush with melted butter, and sprinkle with chopped garlic and pepper. Roll the meat tightly, sew together the ends and tie with string. Melt some butter in a frying pan, add the chicken roll and a bit of water and bake in the oven for approximately 1 hour, moistening the meat with the cooking liquid. Just before the chicken is done, you may brush it with mayonnaise. Let the roll cool a bit and weight it down for 6 hours. Remove the string. Slice the roll and arrange on a plate with marinated fruit (apples, plums) and parsley or dill. If you like, you can stuff the roll with sliced apple and prunes, with a cheese omelet, or with cooked or fried mushrooms.

Easy chicken liver pate

200 g (7 oz) chicken livers,
200 g (7 oz) cream cheese,
100 g (3.5 oz) good quality liver sausage,
dried onion flakes, lemon juice

Run the chicken livers through a food processor and sauté in a bit of vegetable or olive oil until it changes color from reddish to brown-gray. Allow the livers to cool thoroughly. Put them in a large bowl with the cream cheese, liver sausage, onion flakes (to taste) and lemon juice (to taste — the taste of lemon should be fairly pronounced in the pate). Use a hand mixer to blend thoroughly — at least 10 minutes. Serve on rye or sourdough bread.

Chicken in aspic

500 g (17.5 oz) cooked chicken (deboned)

For the gelatin:
1 glass chicken stock,
1/2 glass water,
1 glass plum compote,
1 heaping tablespoon gelatin

First version: Cube the chicken. Rinse small bowls in cold water. Place pitted plums in each bowl. Place the chicken on top and pour the gelatin over top. Allow to set.

Second version: Slice the chicken and arrange it in a small oval dish. Arrange some pitted plums around the edges of the chicken and cover with the gelatin. Allow to set.

Gelatin: allow it to become saturated in cold water and then add to hot chicken stock.
Heat until the gelatin is dissolved and add the plum compote.

Spicy rolled beef

900 g (31.5 oz) sliced beef,
700 g (24.5 oz) sliced fatty pork,
300 g (10.5 oz) sliced smoked pork,
1-2 cloves garlic, mustard,
1 egg, salt, sugar, pepper, butter

Use slices of beef that are 1 1/2-2 cm (0.6-0.8 inches) thick. Chop garlic and sprinkle half over the meat. Press the garlic into the meat. Sprinkle the meat with salt, sugar and pepper. Brush with mustard. Roll and refrigerate for one hour. The pork slices should be 1 cm (0.4 inches) thick. Tenderize with a meat mallet, sprinkle them with the remaining chopped garlic, salt and pepper, and put them on top of the beef slices. Put a piece of smoked pork at the center of each slice and roll them tightly, tying them with string. Brown them in butter, then put in the oven. Add a bit of hot water and bake, moistening with the cooking water from time to time. When the meat is done, remove from the oven and allow it to cool. Weight it down. Slice it before serving. Decorate with vegetables and parsley or dill.

Liver pate

200 g (7 oz) veal or pork liver,
50 g (1.75 oz) smoked bacon,
25 g (0.875 oz) onion, parsley,
100 g (3.5 oz) butter,
pepper, nutmeg, salt,
5 g (0.175 oz) cognac,
the grated zest of 1 lemon,
5 g (0.175 oz) lemon juice

Wash the livers and remove membrane. Cut into quarters. Sauté them quickly in butter with the diced vegetables (onion, parsley). Add hot water to cover partly, add the salt and pepper and sauté until tender. (The livers are ready when they are no longer reddish inside.) Cool the livers, grind or process in food processor them three times and then press through a sieve. Add the nutmeg, lemon zest and cognac, along with a bit of the sauté liquid, to the meat. Heat the mass, stirring all the while. Put it in a bowl and whip it well with a hand mixer along with some butter and the lemon juice. Serve on rye or sourdough bread.

Marinated liver

600 g (21 oz) liver,
40 g (1.4 oz) flour,
60 g (2.1 oz) butter,
salt, pepper.

For the marinade:
200 g (7 oz) water,
200 g (7 oz) vinegar, 1 carrot, 2 onions,
12-15 g (0.42-0.525 oz) sugar (to taste),
salt

Cut the carrots into sticks and the onions into rings. Put the vegetables in hot water, add salt and boil until the vegetables are soft. Add the vinegar and sugar to taste and cool. You can also add 4 peppercorns and 1 bay leaf to the cooking water if you like.

Rinse the livers, remove the membrane and slice. Tenderize with a meat mallet and sprinkle with salt and pepper. Dredge the livers in flour and brown them in melted butter. When they are cool, pour the marinade over them.

Smoked chicken

1 chicken (1 1/2-2 kg (3-4 1/2 lb)),
30 g (1.05 oz) garlic,
1/2 teaspoon pepper,
1/2 teaspoon white pepper,
1 tablespoon salt,
1/2 teaspoon sugar,
1/3 teaspoon lemon juice,
4-5 juniper berries

Choose a young and meaty chicken for this dish. Cut open the chest of the chicken, rub it all over with the salt and spices. Put it in a dish, weight it down and marinate for 2 days in the refrigerator. Smoke the chicken (first at 80 degrees Celsius, and then at 50-60 degrees Celsius), using alder wood and branches for the smoking.

When the chicken is smoked, cut out the backbone and cut off the wing tips. Discard them. Cut the chicken into strips. Arrange the strips on a dish and decorate with marinated fruit and leek leaves. The chicken can also be decorated with fresh berries (strawberries or currants), or with yellow flower blossoms. Duck and goose can be prepared in the same way.

Veal croquettes

3 slices of veal of equal size (150 g (5.25 oz) each),
3 hard-boiled eggs,
1 boiled carrot,
60 g (2.1 oz) smoked or regular bacon,
1 pickle,
salt, pepper, butter

Tenderize the slices of veal on one side with a meat mallet so that slices are 1 cm (0.4 inches) thick. Sprinkle with salt and pepper and arrange slices of bacon, carrot and pickle on top of the meat. Slice the eggs and arrange on top of the bacon and vegetables. Roll the meat tightly and tie or sew it with white thread and string. Put the croquettes in melted butter and brown. Add some water to a baking pan and put meat into the oven for 30-40 minutes. Shortly before the croquettes are cooked, sprinkle them with salt. Cool the croquettes and weight them down lightly for 6 hours. Remove the string and thread, slice the croquettes, arrange them on a shallow plate and decorate with parsley or dill. Croquettes can be prepared with lean pork or rabbit.

Rolled beef

1.2 kg (42 oz) sliced beef,
300 g (10.5 oz) ground pork,
100 g (3.5 oz) dried plums,
4 eggs,
4 tablespoons milk,
3 tablespoons tomato puree,
1 potato,
salt, pepper, nutmeg, sugar, butter

Get beef slices which are 1 cm (0.4 inch) thick. Tenderize on one side only with a meat mallet. Sprinkle with salt, pepper and sugar and brush with tomato puree. Cook eggs into an omelet. Slice and place it on top of the beef slices. Grate the potato. Ad ground pork to the grated potato, nutmeg, salt and pepper. Place on to beef slices. Soak the plums and put them on top of the ground pork. Roll the slices, tie them with string and sauté them in butter until they are browned. Put the slices in the oven and sprinkle them with hot water. When the slices are cooked, cool slightly and weight them down. When completely cool, slice and arrange on a plate. Decorate with marinated pumpkin, apples or plums, and with parsley or dill.

Beef tongue in aspic

400 g (14 oz) boiled beef tongue,
1-2 carrots,
400 g (14 oz) beef stock,
1 pickle,
2 teaspoons of gelatin

Saturate the gelatin with water and then dissolve it in hot beef stock. Put a bit of stock in an oval dish and let it set. Arrange slices of tongue and pickle on top of the gelatin. On both sides of the dish, arrange decoratively cut pieces of carrot. Allow the remaining liquid to set a bit and pour it over the tongue and vegetables.

SAVORY CREAMS
AND
BUTTER CREAMS

Mushroom and ham cream

200 g (7 oz) cooked mushrooms,
200 g (7 oz) sautéed ham,
100 g (3.5 oz) cheese,
100 g (3.5 oz) butter,
4 tablespoons sour cream,
salt, black pepper

Grind or process mushrooms and ham well. Grate the cheese. Lightly whip the butter and add the mushrooms, ham, cheese, salt, peppers and sour cream to it. Mix thoroughly. You may also add 200 g (7 oz) of chopped boiled carrot.

Hot-smoked mackerel cream

1 smoked mackerel,
50 g (1.75 oz) cheese,
100 g (3.5 oz) butter

Remove filets from the mackerel to get 100 g (3.5 oz) of fish. Grind or process the fish. Lightly whip the butter. Grate the cheese. Mix all three ingredients thoroughly. Add 1 tablespoon of horseradish if you like.

Herring and bacon cream

1-2 herring,
100 g (3.5 oz) smoked bacon,
1 medium-tart apple,
1 onion,
1 pickle,
1 boiled potato,
1-2 tablespoons horseradish,
1/2 glass sour cream

Remove filets from the herring and grind or process with potato and bacon. Grate the apple and pickle. Finely chop the onion. Mix all of the ingredients with sour cream and horseradish.

Sprat cream

100 g (3.5 oz) sprat filets,
100 g (3.5 oz) butter

Remove the skins from the sprats and grind them thoroughly, pressing into a solid paste with a mortar and pestle. Whip the butter and mix both ingredients together. Substitute herring for sprats.

41

Cold-smoked mackerel cream

1 smoked mackerel,
100 g (3.5 oz) butter,
1 medium-tart apple,
2 tablespoons spicy tomato sauce,
100 g (3.5 oz) butter

Remove filets from the mackerel to get 100 g (3.5 oz) of fish. Grind or process the fish. Peel the apple and grate it. Lightly whip the butter and add the other ingredients. You may use cheese spread in place of the butter.

Carrot and herring cream

2 herring,
150-200 g (5.25-7 oz) carrots,
50 g (1.75 oz) onion,
100 g (3.5 oz) butter,
1 tablespoon sour cream

Remove filets from herring. Boil the carrots. Grind or process the herring with carrots. Chop the onion and blanch in a little water. Allow to cool. Lightly whip the butter and add all of the ingredients. Mix well.

Green butter

2 tablespoons chopped dill and parsley,
100 g (3.5 oz) butter, lemon juice, salt

Add salt and lemon juice to the chopped parsley or dill and press them into a paste with a mortar and pestle. Whip the butter and add parsley or dill. Mix thoroughly.

Rye bread cream

250 g (8.75 oz) rye bread without the crust,
100 g (3.5 oz) cheese,
100 g (3.5 oz) medium-tart apple,
1 onion,
100 g (3.5 oz) butter,
1-2 tablespoons sour cream,
salt

Finely grate bread, cheese and peeled apple. Chop the onion and blanch in some water. Allow to cool. Lightly whip the butter and add all of the ingredients. Mix well. Spoon the cream into small rounded pieces and roll them in chopped green onion, toasted oats, grated cheese, chopped smoked bacon or fried white bread crumbs. Arrange the rolled pieces of cream on a plate and serve.

Hemp butter

Rinse hemp, dry in a pan over a low flame and toast it a bit (if you toast it too much, the butter will be bitter). Run the hemp through a meat grinder 10 times. Place the mixture into a bowl, add butter and salt.

Mustard butter

20 g (0.7 oz) mustard,
yolks of 2 hard-boiled eggs,
100 g (3.5 oz) butter, salt

Whip the butter and grate the egg yolks. Mix all of the ingredients thoroughly.

Savory torte with smoked mackerel cream

1 loaf rye bread, crusts removed.

Filling:
Cold-smoked and hot-smoked mackerel cream (see above)

For decoration:
Horseradish cream, green butter, mustard butter, green onions

Slice the rye bread horizontally into slices 1/2 cm (0.2 inches) thick. Cut into equal-sized triangles, with one side approximately 4 cm (1.6 inches) in length. You will need nine triangles of bread in all. Place the triangles three apiece into a circle on a plate. Spread the cold-smoked mackerel cream across the triangles. Place another layer of triangles on top. Spread them with the hot-smoked mackerel cream. Place the third layer of bread on top. Press down lightly. Spread more cream around the edges of the torte and sprinkle chopped green onion on the sides, too. Using a cake decorating kit, make roses of horseradish cream, green butter and mustard butter on top of the cake. Substitute dough used in bouillon *pīrāgi* (see index) for rye bread. Bake dough into circles.

Salmon cream

150-200 g (7 oz) smoked or lightly salted salmon,
1/2 glass sweet cream

Whip the cream and grind or process the salmon. Mix the two together. Replace whip cream with sour cream (1/2-3/4 glass).

All of these creams and butters can be used for sandwiches, savory cakes, savory tortes and savory biscuit rolls.

TOASTED SANDWICHES
AND
FRIED BREAD

Fried bread

First version: Remove the crusts from slices of white bread and cube the bread into small cubes. For 50 g (1.75 oz) bread, put 15 g (0.175 oz) butter in a pan and sauté the cubes until they are light brown. The fried cubes can be served with bouillon or soups, putting the cubes in the bowl before the soup is added.

Second version: Rub slices of crustless rye bread with chopped garlic and salt, cut into 1/2 cm (0.2 inches) cubes and sauté in vegetable oil over a high flame (for 50 g (1.75 oz) rye bread, use 5 g (0.175 oz) of garlic and 10 g (0.35 oz) of oil). Serve with beer.

Fried rye bread

First version: Cut the rye bread into slices 1/2 cm (0.2 inches) thick and remove the crusts. Fry in hot vegetable oil on a high flame until crisp.

Second version: Soak slices of crustless rye bread in vegetable oil for a few minutes, rub with chopped garlic and salt, arrange on a baking sheet and bake in a hot oven until crispy.

Fried rye bread with egg

Prepare fried rye bread according to the second version above. Cool, spread with mayonnaise and sprinkle with chopped hard-boiled egg. Place slices of tomato or cucumber on top. Use dried bacon or onions.

Baked cottage cheese sandwiches

50 g (1.75 oz) white bread,
8 g (0.28 oz) butter,
25 g (0.875 oz) dry cottage cheese,
5 g (0.175 oz) sour cream,
1/5 egg (beat a whole egg and take 1/5 of the
*   volume),*
salt, caraway seeds

Mix together the cottage cheese, sour cream, egg, salt and caraway seeds. Slice the bread and cut off its crusts. Butter both sides of the bread and mound the cottage cheese on each slice. Bake in a medium oven until light brown. You may substitute 1 chopped clove of garlic for the caraway seeds.

Baked cheese sandwiches

50 g (1.75 oz) white bread,
15 g (0.525) butter,
20 g (0.7 oz) cheese

First version: Slice white bread, butter the slices, sprinkle a thick layer of grated cheese over the each slice and bake on a baking sheet until the cheese melts. You may add 1 tablespoon of chopped dill or parsley to the cheese.

Second version: Slice white bread, butter the slices, place a slice of cheese on top of each slice and bake on a baking sheet until the cheese melts.

Third version: Slice white bread, butter the slices, cover the slices with diced herring filet or sprat filet, and then sprinkle a thick layer of grated cheese on top. Bake on a baking sheet until the cheese melts.

Fried rye bread with pumpkin and cheese

Lightly salt two slices of pumpkin (1/2 cm or 0.2 inches thick) and sauté in vegetable oil until light brown, turning often. Cut 2 slices of rye bread at the same thickness and sauté in the same oil only on one side. Place bread on a frying pan, uncooked side down. Put the cooked pumpkin on top of the browned side of the bread and cover with slices of cheese. Cover the pan and leave on a slow flame until the cheese begins to melt. Serve warm. Substitute lightly sautéed slices of apple for cheese. Substitute cooked and grated carrot for the pumpkin.

HOT FOODS

SOUPS

Potato and dumpling soup

*800 g (28 oz) good quality beef bouillon
    (preferably home-made with beef bones),
400 g (14 oz) potatoes,
1 carrot,
1 small onion,
parsley root, salt, pepper*

*For the dumplings:
150 g (5.25 oz) boneless beef,
10 g white bread,
10 g onion,
1/2 egg,
10 g fat,
salt, pepper*

Dice carrots, parsley and onion and put them in the beef bouillon. Peel and dice the potatoes and add to the pot. Bring soup to a boil and cook for 10 minutes. Add the dumplings, salt and pepper and cook until the potatoes and dumplings are done.

Dumplings: Soak the bread in water. Chop the onion and sauté lightly in butter. Put the bread, onion and the meat in a meat grinder and grind it twice. Add the egg, salt and pepper and mix well. Shape into dumplings.

Before serving, sprinkle with chopped parsley or dill.

Potato and pickle soup

*150 g (5.25 oz) boneless beef,
800 g (28 oz) water,
20 g (0.7 oz) butter,
30 g (1.05 oz) carrot,
20 g (0.7 oz) onion,
20 g (0.7 oz) parsley and celery root,
400 g (14 oz) potatoes,
50 g (1.75 oz) pickles,
salt, pepper, sour cream, parsley or dill*

Cut the meat against grain into slices 1 1/2 cm (0.6 inches) thick. Tenderize with a meat mallet. Brown in melted butter. Place meat in a pot and cover with boiling water. Dice the onions, carrots, parsley and celery and add them to the pot. Cook until the meat is nearly tender. Add more water if necessary. Peel and dice potatoes. Add them to the soup along with salt and pepper. Cut the pickles lengthwise and remove seeds. When the soup is nearly ready, add the chopped pickles. Heat the pickles thoroughly.

Before serving, cut the slices of meat into bite-sized portions. Add chopped green onions or parsley, and sour cream.

Farmer's soup

200 g (7 oz) smoked pork,
800 g (28 oz) water,
300 g (10.5 oz) potatoes,
30 g (1.05 oz) grouts,
1 onion,
salt, pepper, bay leaves, green onions

Dice the smoked pork and chop onion. Brown in a small pot. Boil the water separately and add it to the pork and onions, along with the grouts. Cook until the grouts and meat are almost tender. Peel and dice the potatoes and add them to the soup, along with salt, pepper and bay leaves. Cook until the potatoes are tender. Use fresh or salted pork. Grits can be substituted for the grouts, but cook them separately until they are semi-tender before adding them to the soup. Before serving, sprinkle with chopped green onion.

Potato and mushroom soup

150 g (5.25 oz) pork,
800 g (28 oz) water,
200 g (7 oz) cooked or salted mushrooms,
400 g (14 oz) potatoes,
30 g (1.05 oz) onion,
30 g (1.05 oz) tomato puree,
pepper, bay leaves, salt, sour cream, green onions

Cut up the pork (whether fresh, salted or smoked) into cubes. Brown pork in butter. Chop mushrooms and onions and add them to the pan, along with the tomato puree. Stir. Cook the mixture for 10 minutes. Boil water separately and add it to the pan. Peel and dice the potatoes and add them to the soup along with salt, pepper and bay leaves. Before serving, sprinkle chopped green onion on the soup and add sour cream.

Fish dumpling soup

800 g (28 oz) fish bouillon,
400 g (14 oz) potato,
30 g (1.05 oz) carrots,
20 g (0.7 oz) onion,
10 g (0.35 oz) parsley,
20 g (0.7 oz) butter,
salt, pepper, bay leaf, parsley or dill

For the dumplings:
150 g (5.25 oz) fish filet (cod, perch, etc.),
20 g (0.7 oz) white bread,
30 g (1.05 oz) milk,
1/2 egg,
pepper, salt

Dice the carrots and potatoes and pour them into the fish bouillon. Bring to a boil and simmer until the potatoes are semi-tender. Meanwhile, sliver the onion and parsley and sauté them for a bit in butter. Add them, along with the fish dumplings, salt, pepper and bay leaf, to the pot. Simmer for 10-15 minutes.

For the dumplings: Remove the crust from the bread and soak in milk. Grind the bread with the fish twice or run them through a food processor. Add the egg, pepper and salt and mix well. Shape into small, round dumplings. Wet your hands before working with dumplings.

47

Sorrel soup

(Note: the dark green sorrel leaf resembles spinach in look and taste. However, sorrel has a lovely tart flavour that can't be replaced in this recipe.)

250 g (8.75 oz) pork,
800 g (28 oz) water,
300 g (10.5 oz) sorrel,
30 g (1.05 oz) carrots,
20 g (0.7 oz) onion,
10 g (0.35 oz) parsley,
20 g (0.7 oz) fat,
20 g (0.7 oz) grits,
salt, sour cream, dill and parsley

Soak the grits for 6-8 hours in cold water. Dice the pork. Pour the pork and the grits in a pot, add water to cover and cook until the meat is almost tender. Chop the sorrel, onions and carrots and sauté them in the butter. Add the vegetables, parsley and salt to the pot, and continue cooking until the meat is tender. Sprinkle with chopped dill or parsley and add sour cream before serving. You may use 200 g (7 oz) of diced potato instead of grits. Boil the potatoes with the cut meat. Steam the sorrel separately and add it to the soup when the meat and potatoes are tender.

Pea soup

250 g (8.75 oz) smoked pork,
800 g (28 oz) water,
80 g (2.8 oz) peas,
30 g (1.05 oz) carrots,

20 g (0.7 oz) onion,
20 g (0.7 oz) grouts,
salt

Soak the grouts in water for 6-8 hours. Cube the meat, pour into a pot and cover with cold water. Bring to a boil, removing any foam. Add the peas (if you use dried peas, soak them thoroughly first) and the grouts. Chop the carrots and onions and add to the soup. Simmer until the meat is tender. Pea soup is traditionally served with meat dishes.

Fresh cabbage soup

300 g (10.5 oz) mutton,
800 g (28 oz) water,
300 g (10.5 oz) fresh cabbage,
200 g (7 oz) potatoes,
1 carrot,
onion,
parsley root,
20 g (0.7 oz) butter,
salt, pepper, bay leaves, parsley or dill

Cut the meat into cubes, pour into a pot. Add cold water to cover and cook on a low flame until the meat is almost tender. Dice the cabbage and add it to the meat. Cook for another 5 minutes. Slice the carrots, parsley and onions and dice the potatoes. Sauté vegetables in butter and add them to the pot, along with salt, pepper and bay leaves. Continue to simmer on a low flame until the meat and vegetables are tender. Add spicy tomato sauce or peeled, seeded and sliced tomato. Sprinkle with parsley or dill before serving.

Sauerkraut soup

> 250 g (8.75 oz) pork (fresh, salted or smoked),
> 800 g (28 oz) water,
> 300 g (10.5 oz) sauerkraut,
> 20 g (0.7 oz) grouts,
> 1 medium onion (chopped),
> 20 g (0.7 oz) butter,
> 20 g (0.7 oz) tomato puree,
> salt, green onion, sour cream

Pour the sauerkraut into a pot and add water. Rinse the grouts and add them to the pot. Dice the pork and add it to the pot. Cook the soup until the sauerkraut and meat are nearly tender. Sauté chopped onion in butter. Add the onion and tomato puree to the soup and cook for another 10-15 minutes.

Sprinkle with chopped green onion and add sour cream to taste before serving.

Hearty bean soup

> 800 g (28 oz) beef or pork bouillon,
> 150 g (5.25 oz) white beans,
> 60 g (2.1 oz) carrots,
> 30 g (1.05 oz) leek or onion,
> 20 g (0.7 oz) parsley,
> 10 g (0.35 oz) flour,
> 20 g (0.7 oz) butter,
> 30 g (1.05 oz) sour cream,
> salt, parsley

Soak the beans in water for 6-8 hours. Sauté choped leek or onion, carrots and parsley in the butter for a bit. Put the vegetables and the beans into the bouillon and cook until the vegetables are tender. Strain the vegetables and beans (reserving the bouillon) and press them through a sieve or puree in a blender or food processor. Return vegetables to bouillon. Sprinkle with flour and stir thoroughly. Simmer slowly for 5-8 minutes. Before serving, add sour cream and some chopped parsley. Traditionally this soup is served with fried white bread or sandwiches. Substitute peas for beans.

Milk soup with fish

> 1/2 l water,
> 1/2 l milk,
> 1/2 kg fish,
> 1/2 kg potato,
> 1 onion,
> salt, parsley, sour cream

Clean and dress the fish. Put the whole fish into a pot, add cold water to cover, salt to taste and simmer over a low flame until the fish is tender. Remove the fish from the soup. Strain the liquid and pour back into the pot. Cube the potatoes and dice the onion. Pour them into the soup and cook until the potatoes are tender. Heat the milk separately and add it to the soup. Remove any bones from the fish and add the fish meat to the pot, as well. Cook until heated through. Before serving, add sour cream, chopped parsley or dill.

Country porridge (*Skābputra*)

600 g (21 oz) water,
40 g (1.4 oz) grouts,
400 g (14 oz) buttermilk or sour milk,
50 g (1.75 oz) sour cream

Rinse the grouts and cook them in boiling water until they are almost tender. Scoop thick buttermilk or sour milk into the water, but do not stir. As the *rūgušpiens* sets, it will form into clumps. Put the porridge in a warm place and allow it to ferment for 12 days. Do not add any salt. Add the sour cream or buttermilk before serving. The "porridge" is traditionally poured into cups and served with sandwiches, herring and boiled potatoes, or with gray peas or pea dumplings.

Milk soup with peas and dropped dumplings

700 g (24.5 oz) milk,
1 glass water,
3/4 glass preserved peas,
10 g (0.35 oz) butter,
salt,
1/2 teaspoon sugar

For the dumplings:

First version:
45 g barley meal,
1 egg,
1 tablespoon milk,
1/2 teaspoon melted butter,
salt to taste

Second version:
45 g barley meal,
1 teaspoon melted butter,
scant half glass milk, 1 egg,
salt, 1 tablespoon chopped dill

In either version, beat the egg thoroughly with salt, the meal (sift it first), melted butter, milk and salt. Stir until air bubbles appear in the dough. Boil the milk and the water. Add the peas, butter, salt and sugar. Drop the dough into the soup by teaspoonful and cook for 2-3 minutes.

Milk soup with blanched dumplings

2 l (2 quarts + 8 tablespoons) milk,
20 g (0.7 oz) butter,
salt to taste

For the dumplings:
1 heaping glass barley meal,
1 glass milk,
50 g (1.75 oz) butter,
3 eggs, salt

To make the dumplings: Boil the milk and melt the butter in it. Add salt and all of the barley meal at once. Quickly stir the dough into a single lump, using a wooden spoon for this purpose. Allow the dough to cool a bit and then add the eggs one by one.

Bring the milk for the soup to a slow boil. Shape dumplings by pressing 2 teaspoons together. Drop the dumplings into the milk and cook them until they rise to the top. Add salt to taste.

You may also cook the dumplings in salted water and serve them in bouillon.

Milk soup with pumpkin and potato

400 g (14 oz) milk,
400 g (14 oz) water,
200 g (7 oz) pumpkin,
150 g (5.25 oz) potato,
50 g (1.75 oz) carrots,
30 g (1.05 oz) butter, salt to taste

Coarsely grate the carrots, put them in a pot with some melted butter and sauté them for a while. Peel and cube the potatoes. Boil the water separately and add it to the pot along with the potatoes and salt to taste. Cook for 5-8 minutes. Meanwhile, cube the pumpkin and add it to the pot. When all of the vegetables are tender, add the milk and return the soup to a boil.

Cold sorrel soup

700 g (24.5 oz) water,
400 g (14 oz) sorrel,
30 g (1.05 oz) green onion,
10 g chopped dill and parsley, 2 eggs,
100 g (3.5 oz) cucumber,
100 g (3.5 oz) sour cream,
salt, sugar

Rinse the sorrel thoroughly and drain. Slice sorrel and steam for 8-10 minutes. Allow it to cool. Chop the green onion, sprinkle with salt and squeeze until soft. Peel, seed and slice the cucumber. Add all of the ingredients except the eggs and the sour cream to the cooled sorrel and mix together. Season to taste. Pour the soup into bowls. In each bowl put half a hard-boiled egg and a scop of sour cream.

Beet soup with fresh cabbage

800 g (28 oz) beef bouillon,
400 g (14 oz) boiled beets,
300 g (10.5 oz) fresh cabbage,
1 carrot, parsley root,
100 g (3.5 oz) potato,
1 tablespoon spicy tomato sauce,
bay leaves, pepper, salt, sugar, lemon juice,
sour cream, 2-3 cloves garlic, parsley or dill

Heat the bouillon. Slice the carrots, chop the parsley. Dice the potatoes and onions. Put them into the bouillon and cook until the vegetables are tender. Grate the beets and heat them thoroughly in a separate pan. Add beets to the pot along with the tomato sauce, salt, pepper, sugar, lemon juice and bay leaves. Cook the ingredients until tender, adding chopped garlic the last moment. Serve with chopped parsley or dill and sour cream.

Cold vegetable soup

800 g (28 oz) water,
300 g (10.5 oz) cauliflower,
100 g (3.5 oz) carrot,
50 g (1.75 oz) fresh peas,
50 g (1.75 oz) cucumber, 1 egg,
100 g (3.5 oz) sour cream,
salt, sugar, chopped dill and parsley

Pour the sliced carrots and cauliflower with the peas into boiling salt water and cook until tender. Let them cool. Slice the cucumber, boil and chop the eggs, and add them to the sour cream, parsley or dill. Pour mixture into soup. Mix thoroughly and cool.

51

Milk soup with potato dumplings

400 g (14 oz) milk,
400 g (14 oz) water

For the dumplings:
1/2 kg (1.2 lb) potato,
70 g (2.45 oz) milk, salt

Peel, rinse and grate the potatoes (as finely as possible so that the dumplings will hold together better). Gather up the mass of potatoes in a double layer of cheesecloth or a linen napkin and squeeze out as much liquid as possible into a bowl. Lay the cheesecloth into another bowl. Heat the milk to boiling and pour it over the potatoes (this will cause them to become lighter in color, and it will remove the taste of raw potato). Add salt to taste along with any potato starch that has risen to the top from the draining of the potatoes earlier. Mix well. Dampen your hands before shaping round dumplings. Boil dumplings in salted water until they are ready. Add the milk from the second bowl and bring to a boil. Try boiling and mashing potatoes with raw egg and sour cream. This will make the dumplings softer and easier to shape.

Milk soup with rubbed dumplings

700 g (24.5 oz) milk,
200 g (7 oz) water,
10 g (0.35 oz) butter,
salt, sugar

For the dumplings:
100 g (3.5 oz) barley meal,
30 g (1.05 oz) milk,
1 egg, salt to taste

Whip together the egg, the salt and the milk. Add approximately 3/4 of the barley meal and stir into a thick dough. Dump the rest of the meal into the bowl and start rubbing the dough with your hands to create small dumplings. You may also use rough-milled wheat or rye flour instead of barley meal.

Boil the water with the milk and add the dumplings. Cook for 3-5 minutes. Add the butter, salt and sugar to taste.

Cold beet soup

500 g (17.5 oz) sour milk or buttermilk,
400 g (14 oz) young beets (roots with the leaves),
70 g (2.45 oz) cucumber, 2 eggs,
50 g (1.75 oz) sour cream,
20 g (0.7 oz) green onion,
dill, salt, sugar to taste

Rinse the beets thoroughly. Cut them into bite-sized pieces, put them in a pot. Pour boiling water over them to cover. Cover the pot and steam the beets. Let them cool.

Beat the buttermilk or sour milk and add the steamed beets with all of the liquid. Add salt and sugar to taste. Peel, seed and dice the cucumber. Boil the eggs and chop. Add them to the soup with chopped green onion, dill and sour cream.

You can also prepare this dish with boiled mature beets. Beat the buttermilk or sour milk with a small amount of the beet cooking liquid (allow it to cool first), along with salt and sugar. Grate the boiled beets, add to the liquid along with chopped, seeded cucumber, chopped radish, a diced hard-boiled egg and chopped green onions and dill. Finally, add the sour cream.

FISH DISHES

Fried fish filet

*300 g (10.5 oz) fish (perch, captain's fish,
    cod, etc.) filets,
salt, black pepper, mustard,
10 g (0.35 oz) flour,
12 g (0.42 oz) dry bread crumbs,
1 egg,
vegetable oil for frying,
20 g (0.7 oz) butter*

Skin the filets and cut them up into bite size pieces. Tenderize with a meat mallet. Sprinkle with salt and pepper, and rub fish with mustard. Let them stand in the refrigerator for 20 minutes. Dredge the fish with flour and the dry bread crumbs. Dip in egg, and brown on both sides. Melt the butter in a separate pan. Serve on a shallow plate and pour the melted butter over it. Serve with baked potatoes and fresh vegetable salad. You may also serve sautéed or cooked chanterelle mushrooms with this dish. For the mushrooms: *1/2 liters chanterelle mushrooms (choose the smallest ones), salt, water.* Rinse the chanterelles in water several times to remove all dirt and sand from them. Leave the stems of the mushrooms on. Add 1 tablespoon of salt to a liter of cold water, put the mushrooms in the water and cook for 30 minutes, until tender. Drain and serve.

Fish cooked in milk

*500 g (17.5 oz) fish (perch, mackerel, etc.),
140 g (4.9 oz) flavoring vegetables (onion,
    parsley, carrot),
260 g (9.1 oz) milk,
2 tablespoons vegetable oil,
salt, pepper, bay leaf,
2 tablespoons sour cream,
chopped parsley or dill*

Cut the fish into pieces, cut the onion into rings, coarsely grate the carrot, and chop the parsley. Layer the fish with the vegetables in a medium-sized pot. Sprinkle vegetable oil, salt and pepper over each layer. Heat the milk in a separate pot, but do not boil. Pour it over the fish and add a bay leaf. Simmer on a low flame for 30 minutes. Remove from the heat and stir in the sour cream.

Serve the fish in with the liquid it was cooked, with boiled potatoes and warm beet salad. Sprinkle the chopped herbs on the fish before serving.

Cod with bacon

500 g (17.5 oz) cod,
3 g smoked bacon,
40 g (1.4 oz) butter,
30 g (1.05 oz) sour cream, salt,
10 g (0.35 oz) flour,
20 g (0.7 oz) cheese

Clean and dress the fish, cut into serving-sized pieces. You should have about 120 g (4.2 oz) of fish when you have removed all of the bones. Rub slices of smoked bacon over the fish. Melt butter in an ovenproof pan. Place the fish in the pan and bake it in the oven for 10 minutes. Pour 1-2 glasses of hot water into the pan (do not cover the fish fully) and sauté for another 15 minutes. Grate the cheese and sprinkle over the fish. Sauté for another 5 minutes. Remove the fish from the pan and arrange it on a shallow plate. Serve with boiled potatoes and warm beet salad. Prepare a sauce using the cooking liquid. For the sauce: Heat flour in a dry pan. Add the sour cream and mix well. Pour in a little fish broth. Stir it well, and add to the remaining cooking liquid. Salt to taste and simmer until thickened.

Fried fish in batter

500 g (17.5 oz) fish (perch, pike, etc.) filet,
vegetable oil

For the marinade:
10 g (0.35 oz) vegetable oil,
50 g (1.75 oz) vinegar,
salt, sugar, pepper, chopped parsley

For the sauce:
160 g (5.6 oz) fish stock,
8 g (0.28 oz) flour,
50 g (1.75 oz) butter,
8 g (0.28 oz) onion,
6 g (0.21 oz) parsley,
1/2 egg yolk,
20 g (0.7 oz) dry white wine,
salt, lemon juice

For the batter:
100 g (3.5 oz) milk or beer,
10 g (0.35 oz) vegetable oil,
2 eggs,
150 g (5.25 oz) flour, salt

Skin the filets and cut them 1 cm (0.4 inches) thick and 5-6 cm (2-2.4 inches) long. Whisk together all of the ingredients for the marinade, pour it over the fish, cover and refrigerate for 12 hours. Dip the fish pieces into the batter and deep fry them until they are browned. Drain and arrange in a warmed bowl. Serve with baked potatoes, fresh vegetable salad (tomatoes, cucumbers, lettuce) and the fish sauce.

For the dough: Separate the eggs. Mix together milk or beer with the egg yolks, salt, vegetable oil and flour until you get a smooth dough. Whip the egg whites until foamy and fold them into the dough.

For the sauce: Heat the flour in 30 g (1.05 oz) of the butter, add the fish stock, stir thoroughly and simmer for 15-20 minutes. Add salt and lemon juice to taste. Cut up the onion and parsley. Sauté in butter, add the sauce to the pan and simmer for 15 minutes. Strain the sauce, add the egg yolk and white wine, and return to the heat. Heat through, stirring often.

Herring with cottage cheese and boiled potatoes

1 herring,
100 g (3.5 oz) dry cottage cheese,
25 g (0.875 oz) sour cream, salt,
250 g (8.75 oz) boiled potatoes,
green onion

For one person: Dress the herring and remove the filets. Cut the filets on a diagonal, in long pieces and arrange them on a shallow plate. Mix the cottage cheese with the sour cream and salt to taste, and serve with boiled potatoes. Sprinkle chopped green onion over the herring before serving.

Fish baked with mayonnaise

600 g (21 oz) cod filet,
quince or lemon juice, salt,
3 onions,
100 g (3.5 oz) mild white cheese,
200 g (7 oz) mayonnaise,
2 tablespoons chopped parsley,
butter or vegetable oil

Slice the filets lengthwise and sprinkle them with the quince or lemon juice and salt. Slice the onions into thin rounds. Heat butter or vegetable oil in a heavy pan, add the fish and turn to brown on all sides. Sprinkle the onion and spread mayonnaise over the fish in the pan, bake in the oven for 15 minutes. Grate the cheese, sprinkle it over the fish, and bake for another 5 minutes. Before serving, sprinkle with chopped parsley. Serve with mashed potatoes and baked rutabaga.

Baked carp

600 g (21 oz) carp,
40 g (1.4 oz) butter,
10 g (0.35 oz) garlic,
salt,
100 g (3.5 oz) sour cream

Clean and wash the fish, but do not dress it. Cut the fish, complete with skin and bones, into round serving-sized pieces. Chop garlic and rub it over the fish, sprinkle with salt. Melt butter in an ovenproof pan. Place the fish pieces in the pan, add the sour cream, and bake in the oven for 20-25 minutes. Serve with boiled potatoes and fresh vegetables.

Fish cakes

400 fish filet,
2 tablespoons manna-croupt,
1-2 eggs,
2 tablespoons sweet cream,
1 small onion,
1/2 teaspoon butter,
salt, pepper, dry bread crumbs, vegetable oil

Remove the skins from the filets and grind them twice. Chop the onion and simmer with melted butter over medium heat. Add the onion to the fish and grind again. Add salt, pepper, eggs, manna-croup and cream to the ground fish and mix well. Shape into small cakes. Dredge fish in bread crumbs and sauté in vegetable oil until they are brown. Bake in a hot oven for 5 minutes before serving. Serve with mashed potatoes and onion or mushroom sauce.

Fish dumplings for children

*200 g (7 oz) fish filet, 1 egg yolk, 1 tablespoon
sweet cream, 1 tablespoon manna-croup,
1 tablespoon chopped parsley or dill, 1 tablespoon melted butter, salt*

Grind the fish filets twice. Add the egg
yolk, manna-croup, parsley or dill, cream, butter
and salt. Mix thoroughly. Shape into small
dumplings. Boil them in water for 15-20 minutes. You can also use the fish for fish cakes,
dredge in flour, brown in butter, and then bake
in a hot oven, as in the previous recipe. Serve
with boiled cauliflower. Add grated vegetables
(carrots or potatoes) to the cooking water before
you add the fish dumplings.

Grilled herring

Clean and dress salted herring, removing
their insides and cutting off the heads and tails.
Soak the herring in water, wrap it in baking
paper and grill over hot coals. When the fish is
ready, carefully peel away the paper. Serve with
potatoes boiled in their jackets, sour cream and
chopped green onion.

Fish dumplings stuffed with pork

*300 g (10.5 oz) fish filet,
1 egg,
1 tablespoon manna-croup,
1 tablespoon cheese spread,
1 small onion,
salt, nutmeg, pepper, vegetable oil*

For the stuffing:
*150 g (5.25 oz) ground pork (it can be smoked
pork),
salt, pepper*

Slice the filets and chop until they form a
paste. Beat the egg and add it to the fish, along
with the cheese spread, spices and manna-croup.
Mix well. Divide the fish into four portions.
Flatten each portion on a board. Place some of
the ground pork, salted and peppered to taste, in
the center of each circle. Fold up the edges and
press. Heat some oil in a pan, add the stuffed
dumplings. Bake in the oven for 10 minutes. Add
1/2 glass fish stock or water and sauté for
another 15 minutes. Serve with boiled carrots,
rutabagas or cauliflower.

MEAT DISHES

Baked pork ribs (for 10 servings)

*1 1/2-2 kg (3.2-4.3 lb) pork (the side, with
    ribs intact),
50 g (1.75 oz) onion,
50 g (1.75 oz) carrot,
25 g (0.875 oz) chopped parsley,
salt, pepper*

Cut the membrane across each of the ribs (at the side of pork), so that the meat can be removed easily after baking. Rub the meat with salt and pepper and cook it as you would a pork roast. If the meat is fatty, remove the skin and some of the fat. When the meat is ready, cut into serving-sized pieces (two ribs per serving) and put it into a serving bowl. Keep the meat warm. Make a sauce from the pork drippings and pour it over the meat. Serve with boiled or baked potatoes and vegetable salad.

Pork ribs with horseradish sauce

*1/2kg (1.1 lb) pork (the side, with ribs intact)
    from a piglet,
50 g (1.75 oz) onion,
2 cloves garlic,
1 carrot,
parsley,
pepper, 4 cloves, bay leaf, salt*

Grind the cloves. Chop up the onion, garlic and bay leaf. Mix together cloves, onion, garlic, salt, pepper and bay leaf. Rub this mixture over the meat. Cover and keep in the refrigerator for 10-12 hours. Rinse the meat, cut the membrane above the ribs (after cooking the ribs will fall away from the meat easily), and put the meat into a large pot of boiling water. Return to a boil, remove any foam, add the flavoring vegetables (chop them first), and simmer on a low flame until the meat is tender. Remove meat from the bouillon. Reserve the liquid. Remove the ribs and cube the meat into bite-sized pieces. Place the meat in a deep dish and serve with horseradish sauce, boiled potatoes or beans and pickles. Substitute pork ribs with pork chops.

*For the horseradish sauce:
200 g (7 oz) of the liquid in which the meat
    was cooked
8 g (0.28 oz) flour;
30 g (1.05 oz) butter;
2 teaspoons horseradish, lemon juice, salt, sugar*

Put the flour and butter in a pan and heat through. Add the bouillon and some salt, and simmer the liquid over a low flame for 10 minutes, stirring often. Add sugar, salt and lemon juice to taste. Add the horseradish. Stir thoroughly.

Stuffed rolled pork

250 g (8.75 oz) good-quality pork,
salt, egg, dry bread crumbs, fat

For the stuffing:
50 g (1.75 oz) ground fatty pork,
50 g (1.75 oz) ground beef,
1-2 cloves garlic,
1 small onion,
25 g (0.875 oz) white bread,
1 teaspoon sweet cream,
salt, pepper

Slice the meat into four pieces. Tenderize with a meat mallet and sprinkle with salt. Put some of the stuffing on each piece, roll up tightly, dip in the beaten egg, dredge in dry bread crumbs and brown in a pan. Put the meat in a pot, smother it with white sauce (see below), and simmer on a low flame for 15 minutes.

Serve with boiled or mashed potatoes, along with the sauce in which the rolled pork was sautéed.

To make the stuffing: Grind process the beef. Grind it again adding the pork and white bread (soaked in water and squeezed to remove most of the liquid). Add to the ground meat chopped onion and garlic, along with salt, pepper, the cream and one tablespoon of water.

For the white sauce:
200 g (7 oz) beef or chicken stock,
30 g (1.05 oz) butter,
onion or leek,
parsley root,
10 g (0.35 oz) flour,
sugar, salt, lemon juice, chopped parsley or dill

Chop the onion or leek, and the parsley root and sauté in butter. Add flour all at once and stir until mixed together. Add the stock, salt to taste, and simmer slowly for 10-15 minutes, stirring occasionally. Strain the liquid. Run the vegetables through a sieve and return to the pot, along with the lemon juice (mixed in some water and sugar). Bring to a boil. Add two teaspoons of butter and the chopped parsley or dill and stir.

Baked smoked ham (for 10 servings)

1 1/2-2 kg (3.2-4.3 lb) smoked ham,
0.8-1 kg (1.8-2.2 lb) rough-milled rye flour,
water

Soak the smoked ham in cold water for 8-10 hours to soften the outer skin and to remove some of the salt. Make a thick dough from the flour, adding enough water for this purpose. Roll out the dough on a hard surface until it is 1-1 1/2 cm (0.4-0.6 inches) thick. Dry the soaked ham and wrap it in the dough. Put the bundle in a roasting pan with the fattier side of the ham on top. Place in a medium oven and bake for 2-2.5 hours. Sprinkle water over the dough from time to time to keep it from burning (you can use a spray bottle for this purpose). When the meat is ready, cool on a rack before taking off the dough. Slice the meat and serve with boiled or baked potatoes and sauerkraut salad. You may also prepare fresh or salted ham like this.

Grout or country sausage

500 g (17.5 oz) medium-ground barley
grouts,
1 1/2-2 l (1 1/2 — 2 quarts) pork bouillon,
250 g (8.75 oz) pork (from the side or head),
1 l (1 quart + 4 tablespoons) pig's blood,
75-100 g (3.5 oz) onion,
100 g (3.5 oz) lard,
salt, pepper, ground cloves, thyme, marjoram,
100 g (3.5 oz) fat for frying

Boil the pork until it is tender. Remove it from the liquid and dice the meat into small pieces. Return the cooking liquid to a boil. Rinse the grouts and boil them in the bouillon, stirring occasionally, until the grouts are almost tender and you have a fairly thick porridge. Let the porridge cool, then pour in the pig's blood through a sieve. Chop the onion and sauté in butter. Add it to the meat. Chop fresh herbs. Add salt, pepper, ground cloves and herbs to the meat. Mix well. Fill the stuffing into sausage casings, about three-quarters full. (If casings are over-stuffed completely, they can burst during cooking.) Tie up the ends of the casings so that the sausage is in the form of a circle. Boil the sausages in salted water, and then heat them over a low flame for a while. Sausages are ready, when you prick them with fork, and the liquid runs clear. Before serving the sausages, brown them in the frying fat, either on top of the stove or in the oven. Traditionally they are served with loganberry preserves.

Roast pork (10 servings)

1 1/2-2 kg (3.2-4.3 lb) pork (ham, shoulder
or back),
1 onion,
salt, pepper

Rub the meat with salt and pepper. Put it skin side down in a roasting pan. Add water to cover the skin, and bake in the oven until the skin is soft and the water has almost evaporated. Turn the meat over and use a sharp knife to cut the skin in many squares. (This will make it easier to cut.) Put the meat back in the roasting pan, add boiling water and chopped onion, and roast in a medium oven for 1-2 hours, basting often. If the pork is tough, boil it in water until almost tender before scoring the skin and roasting the pork in the oven. If the pork is boneless, tie it tightly with string before roasting.

Slice the roast, arrange it in a bowl, pour some of the cooking liquid over it and serve with baked potatoes, sautéed cabbage or baked potatoes. You may also let the roast cool and then serve it cold with slices of baked apple, marinated fruit or fresh vegetables.

Fried liver

First version:
300 g (10.5 oz) pork or beef liver,
salt, pepper, flour,
vegetable oil for frying,
150 g (5.25 oz) onion,
150 g (5.25 oz) apple, butter

Pour skim milk over the liver to cover and set aside in the refrigerator for 2-3 hours. Strain the liver and remove any membrane. Dress the liver and cut into thick slices (approximately 6 cm (2.4 inches) in thickness). Tenderize with a meat mallet. Sprinkle with salt and pepper, dredge in flour. Melt vegetable oil in a frying pan and fry the livers for 4-5 minutes, turning them occasionally. (Liver is ready when there is no more pink inside them.) While the liver is frying, peel and core the apple and cut it into thin rings. Also cut the onion into rings. In a separate pan, sauté the onion and apple in some butter until soft (watch the apples carefully — do not let the rings fall apart!). Put the liver in a large bowl and cover with the sautéed onion and apple. Serve with baked or boiled potatoes.

Second version:
300 g (10.5 oz) liver,
2 tablespoons butter,
1 teaspoon flour, 2 onions,
1 glass sour cream,
salt, pepper

Dress the liver and cut into slices that are 5 cm (2 inches) thick. Then cut each of the slices into strips that are 1 cm (0.4 inches) wide and 6 cm (2.4 inches) long. Sprinkle with salt and pepper and dredge the liver in the flour. Melt the butter in a pan and quickly brown the liver on all sides. Chop the onions and sauté them in a separate pan, also in butter. Put the liver and onions into a pot, pour in sour cream, simmer over a low flame. Do not overcook the liver, or it will become hard. Serve with boiled potatoes and marinated or baked apples.

Roast piglet (10-15 servings)

1 piglet (2-3 kg (4.3-6.5 lb) in weight),
80 g (2.8 oz) butter,
40 g (1.4 oz) sour cream,
salt, carrots

Dress the piglet, chopping the ribs in half lengthwise and scoring some cuts in the shoulder and ham parts of the piglet, along the backbone. Rub the inside of the piglet with salt and spread sour cream (or olive oil) over the skin. Slice the carrots and lay them in the bottom of a roasting pan. Put the piglet on top of the carrots and brush with melted butter. Poke the skin of the piglet with a fork in several places, which will keep the skin from bubbling up during the roasting. Wrap the head and tail of the piglet with tin foil to keep them from burning. Add 1/2 glass water to the pan.

First roast the piglet at a temperature of 200-250°C (392-482°F), and when the skin is browned, lower the temperature to 170-180°C (338-356°F). During the roasting, baste with liquid from time to time. Serve slices of the piglet with baked potatoes, marinated apples and mushroom sauce.

Pork chops (for 2 servings)

300 g (10.5 oz) pork chops,
salt, pepper, 1/2 egg,
dry bread crumbs,
fat (or vegetable oil) for frying,
butter

Tenderize the pork chops with a meat mallet until they are relatively flat. Slice them lengthwise first if they are thick. Sprinkle with salt and pepper, dip in beaten egg, dredge in dry bread crumbs and fry over a medium flame until the meat is browned on both sides for at least 15 minutes. (Meat should be white not pink on the inside.) Pour melted butter over the chops before serving. Serve with baked potatoes and sautéed sauerkraut.

Pork and cabbage patties

150 g (5.25 oz) fatty ground pork,
150 g (5.25 oz) fresh cabbage,
1 1/2 egg, 1 onion,
1 tablespoon almost cooked rice,
salt, pepper, flour, butter,
1 glass spicy tomato sauce,
1/2 glass water

Grate cabbage and chop the onion. Add to the ground pork, along with the egg, salt, pepper and rice. Mix well. Shape the pork into small or larg patties, as you like. Dredge the patties in flour. Melt some butter in a frying pan and brown the patties on all sides. Put them in a pot, pour the spicy tomato sauce over them, along with the water, and simmer gently for 10-15 minutes.

Rolled beef

200 g (7 oz) good-quality beef (from the flank),
salt, sugar, pepper,
butter,
carrot,
parsley,
onion,
20 g (0.7 oz) flour,
sour cream

For the filling:
80 g (2.8 oz) smoked bacon,
40 g (1.4 oz) rye bread,
40 g (1.4 oz) onion,
toothpicks

Cut the beef into slices 1 cm (0.4 inches) thick and are as long as possible. Tenderize the beef with a meat mallet. Sprinkle with salt, sugar and pepper. Put a heaping teaspoonful of filling on one end of each slice and roll the beef up tightly, fastening it with toothpicks. Melt butter and brown rolls in a frying pan, with the wrapping side down. Put the rolls in a large pot, cover with hot water or beef stock. Add the onion, carrot and parsley and sauté until done.

Put the rolls in a deep dish and smother them with a sauce that you prepare from the cooking liquid. Serve with boiled potatoes and pickles.

For the filling: Finely dice the smoke bacon and chop the onion. Sauté in a pan. Grate or finely dice the rye bread and add it to the bacon and onion. Heat mixture through one more time before rolling the beef.

61

Beef patties (*kotletes*)

400 g (14 oz) ground beef,
100 g (3.5 oz) white bread,
onion,
1 clove garlic,
1/2 glass water,
1 tablespoon sour cream,
1 teaspoon butter,
1/2 teaspoon salt,
1/4 teaspoon sugar,
pepper,
1/2 teaspoon potato starch,
butter for frying

Soak the white bread in water and press it to remove most of the liquid. Chop the onion and sauté in melted butter. Mix together the meat, the bread and the onion and run it through a meat grinder for a second time. Chop the garlic and add it and all of the other ingredients to the meat. Mix together well. Refrigerate for 1 hour. Shape the meat into thick oval patties and roll them in dry bread crumbs or flour (this is optional — the patties can also be made without breading). In a castiron pan melt the butter and brown patties on both sides. Then put them in a hot oven and bake for a few minutes more.

You may also stuff the patties: Press patties to make them flat. Fill them with finely diced bacon that you have sautéed together with some chopped onion. You may also prepare an omelet with parsley, finely dice the eggs and use it for the stuffing. Fold over the patties, press together the edges, dredge them in dry bread crumbs and prepare as above.

Serve the patties with a brown gravy, mashed potatoes and sautéed vegetables.

Beef with onion in cream sauce

300 g (10.5 oz) good-quality beef (from the
*   flank or back),*
salt, pepper,
butter,
200 g (7 oz) onion,
300 g (10.5 oz) melted butter,
water or beef stock,
1 heaping teaspoon flour,
100 g (3.5 oz) sour cream

Slice the beef and tenderize it with a meat mallet. Sprinkle with salt and pepper. Press the slices down to make flat, rounded forms and brown them quickly in melted butter over a high flame. Put the browned beef into a pot and cover it with water or beef stock. Cover the pot and sauté the beef until it is tender. About 15 minutes before the beef is ready, slice the onion into rings and sauté in butter. In another pan, heat the flour over a low flame and then add the sour cream, mixing well. Add the onion and the sour cream mixture to the pot, recover and sauté for another 15-20 minutes. Put the meat and the sauce in a deep dish and serve with boiled potatoes and pickles.

Ground beef sauce

*300 g (10.5 oz) good quality ground beef
(from the flank or shoulder),*
75 g (2.625 oz) smoked bacon,
50 g (1.75 oz) onion,
15 g (5.25g) flour,
150 g (5.25 oz) water or beef stock,
75 g (2.625 oz) sour cream,
salt, green onion, parsley

Finely dice the bacon and onion and sauté them in a large frying pan. Add the ground beef stirring, for 4-5 minutes. Boil the water or beef stock in a separate pot. Add it to the meat, along with the flour (heated first in a small pan), salt and sour cream. You may also add some spicy tomato sauce. Simmer for 8-10 minutes. Place the sauce in a deep dish and sprinkle with chopped green onion or parsley. Serve with boiled or mashed potatoes and pickles.

Brown gravy

400 g (14 oz) beef stock,
60 g (2.1 oz) butter,
60 g (2.1 oz) carrot,
40 g (1.4 oz) onion,
10 g (0.35 oz) parsley,
10 g (0.35 oz) celery,
20 g (0.7 oz) flour,
salt, pepper, bay leaf

Dice all of the vegetables and sauté them in butter. Add the flour all at once and stir thoroughly. Simmer for 15-20 minutes, stirring frequently. Strain the sauce and press the vegetables through a sieve. Return vegetables to the liquid. Add another 20 g (0.7 oz) of butter and heat, stirring, until the butter is melted.

Boiled beef tongue (6 servings)

1 beef tongue (0.8-1 kg (1.8-2.2 lb)),
parsley,
celery,
1 onion,
5 peppercorns,
3 white peppercorns,
1 bay leaf,
1 clove,
salt,
butter

Rinse the tongue several times in warm water. Put the tongue in a sieve and pour boiling water over it. Add enough water in a pot to cover the meat, and bring to a boil. Peel the onion and press the clove into it. Put the onion, clove, salt, parsley, celery, bay leaf and the peppercorns into the pot, too. Simmer over a low flame for 2-3 hours. When the tongue is done, rinse in cool water. Remove the membrane and cut the tongue into slices 1 cm (0.4 inches) thick. Sauté in melted butter, and serve with mashed potatoes, peas, horseradish or sour cream sauce.

Meatloaf (8 servings)

800 g (28 oz) boneless beef,
200 g (7 oz) smoked bacon,
120 g (4.2 oz) white bread,
240 g (8.4 oz) water or milk,
80 g (2.8 oz) onion,
160 g (5.6 oz) butter,
40 g (1.4 oz) potato starch,
salt, pepper,
40 g (1.4 oz) dry bread crumbs

Soak bread in milk or water. Grind the bread and beef together twice. Chop the onion and sauté in butter. Add the bread, the remaining water or milk, the onion, the potato starch, the salt and the pepper and mix thoroughly. Dice the smoked bacon into fine dice and add to the meat. With damp hands shape the meat into a loaf that is 5-6 cm (2-2.4 inches) in diameter. Roll it in breadcrumbs. Melt the butter in a loaf pan. Put the loaf in the pan and bake in the oven until it is browned. Add some boiling water or beef stock to the pan and continue to bake the meatloaf until it is ready. Baste with butter while it is baking.

When the meatloaf is ready, allow it to cool. Slice and arrange it on a shallow plate, and serve with cream sauce, boiled potatoes, pickles or fresh vegetable salad.

Latgale sausages

700 g (24.5 oz) lean pork,
200 g (7 oz) beef,
100 g (3.5 oz) bacon,
caraway seeds, salt, pepper, sugar,
3/4 glass water, sausage casings

Grind or process the pork and beef twice. Dice the bacon and grind the caraway seeds in a spice grinder. Mix together all of the ingredients and set aside for 2 hours in the refrigerator. Stuff sausage casings with the mixture and tie up the ends. You may smoke the sausages or bake them in an oven, occasionally sprinkling them with water. Serve with sautéed sauerkraut and boiled potatoes.

Mock partridge

600 g (21 oz) good-quality veal,
100 g (3.5 oz) smoked bacon,
40 g (1.4 oz) fat,
1 onion,
1 carrot,
1/2 parsley root,
1 tablespoon flour,
60 g (2.1 oz) sour cream,
salt

Slice the veal. Tenderize with a meat mallet and sprinkle with salt. Place a slice of bacon on top of each piece of veal and fold it over or roll it up, fastening it with a toothpick. Brown the meat in some hot fat, then put it in a pot and cover it with hot water. Add the chopped vegetables with salt to taste, to the pot. Sauté the meat until tender.

Remove the meat from the liquid and make a sauce with the cooking liquid, adding flour and sour cream. Serve the meat with boiled potatoes or rice and a fresh vegetable salad.

Oven-baked potatoes

HOT FOODS

Latgale sausages with sautéed sauerkraut

Herring with cottage cheese and boiled potatoes

Fried fish filet

Baked carp

Beef patties (*kotletes*) with mashed grated potatoes

Veal schnitzel with sautéed carrots and peas

Pork chops

Rolled beef

Baked pork ribs

Sautéed chicken

Sautéed rabbit

Roast pork

COUNTRY HOLIDAYS

Information and reservations of B&B accommodations, vacation cottages, hotels and guesthouses in countrysides of Latvia, Lithuania, Estonia.

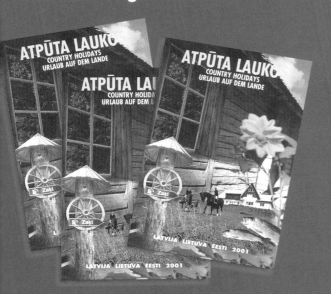

Request our annual catalogue COUNTRY HOLIDAYS

and ACTIVE HOLIDAYS IN LATVIA - a map for independent travellers. Tourist accommodations, touring routes, fishing and horseback riding facilities, nature friendly holiday options in Latvia.

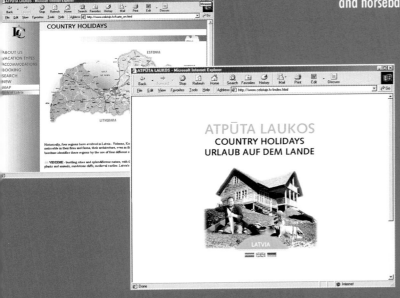

Welcome to our office:

Latvian Country Tourism Association

LAUKU CEĻOTĀJS

11, Kuģu str., Riga, LV-1048

Open: weekdays 10.00. a.m. till 6.00 p.m.

Tel: +371 7617600; e-mail: lauku@celotajs.lv

Visit the country holidays web site http://www.traveller.lv

Oskars

You will always find
a wide choice
of international dishes
and a perfect banquet service
in restaurant OSKARS.

grilbārs
Bruno

A good choice
of beer and a special menu
in our pub BRUNO.

Hotel Amrita is your place for:

- business
- leisure
- conferences
- family holidays

HOTEL
AMRITA

Rigas iela 7/9, Liepaja, LV 3401, Latvia, Phone +371 34 03434, Fax +371 34 80444
www.amrita.lv

Caraway seed sausage (10 servings)

1 kg (2 lb, 3 oz) ground pork,
2 glasses oats (not instant oats),
1 egg,
1/2 glass spicy tomato sauce,
3/4 glass water,
2 teaspoons salt,
pepper,
2 tablespoons ground caraway seeds,
1/2 tablespoon regular caraway seeds,
4 cloves garlic

Mix all of the ingredients together (chopping the garlic first). Set aside in the refrigerator for 12 hours. Shape the meat into sausages — 8 to 10 cm (3.2-4 inches) long and approximately the width of an adult's thumb. Grease a baking sheet. Put the "sausages" on a pan and broil in a hot oven for 15-20 minutes. Serve with salad.

Kurzeme sausage

500 g (17.5 oz) pork,
250 g (8.75 oz) beef,
150-200 g (5.25-7 oz) water,
pepper,
ground ginger,
caraway seeds,
sausage casing

In separate dished, finely dice the pork and beef. Sprinkle with salt and cover. Refrigerate for 10-12 hours. Grind the pork once and the beef two or three times. Add the water, pepper, ginger and caraway seeds to the beef and knead thoroughly. Add the pork and mix well.

Fill the meat into thin sausage casings to form sausages 10-12 cm (4-4.8 inches) long. Smoke them at a temperature of 70-75°C (158-167°F) and let them cool. Before serving, put the sausages in boiling, salted water and simmer over a low flame for 10 minutes. Serve the sausages with sautéed sauerkraut.

Lamb sausages

500 g (17.5 oz) ground lamb kidney,
3 onions,
4 cloves garlic,
3 eggs,
1-1 1/2 tablespoons flour,
salt, pepper, caraway seeds,
40 g (1.4 oz) butter

Mix ground kidney with salt and set aside in the refrigerator for 8-10 hours. Grind the meat again and add the eggs and flour. Chop the onion and garlic and sauté them in butter. Let cool. Add to the meat and mix well. Heat the caraway seeds in a pan and add them to the meat, along with pepper. Mix well and set aside in the refrigerator for 4-5 hours. Wet hands to shape the meat into small, thin sausages 3-4 cm (1.2-1.6 inches) long. Place the sausages in a greased pan and bake in the oven for 10-15 minutes. Serve hot with rye bread and vegetable salad.

Veal schnitzel (2 servings)

First version:
250 g (8.75 oz) good-quality veal,
salt, pepper, butter,
30 g (1.05 oz) mild white cheese, 1 egg,
1 tablespoon sour cream,
1 heaping tablespoon flour,
1 tablespoon chopped parsley or dill

Cut the veal into two slices. Tenderize it with a meat mallet, sprinkle salt and pepper. Brown in hot butter. Grate the cheese and mix with egg, sour cream, flour and parsley or dill. Pour the mixture over the slices of veal and bake in the oven. Serve with baked potatoes and boiled and then sautéed cauliflower.

Second version:
250 g (8.75 oz) good-quality veal,
mustard, salt, sugar,
40 g (1.4 oz) butter

For the batter:
1 egg,
1 tablespoon flour,
1 tablespoon milk, salt

Cut the veal into 2 slices. Tenderize it with a meat mallet. Rub with mustard, sprinkle with salt and sugar. Set aside for 12 hours in the refrigerator. Brown the meat in hot butter.

Beat the egg and mix with flour, milk and salt. When the meat is browned, allow it to cool thoroughly. Dredge in flour, dip it in the batter and sauté in butter until ready. Battered schnitzel can be served hot or cold with loganberry preserves.

Sautéed lamb with vegetables

200 g (7 oz) good-quality mutton,
50 g (1.75 oz) vegetable oil,
1 carrot,
1 onion,
200 g (7 oz) cabbage,
200 g (7 oz) potato,
1/2 glass spicy tomato sauce,
salt, pepper, sugar,
1 teaspoon flour,
1/8 glass sour cream,
chopped herbs

Divide the meat into four equal portions. Melt vegetable oil in a roasting pan. Chop the onion, dice the carrots and cut the cabbage into large pieces. Place the meat, onion, tomato sauce, salt, sugar, carrot and cabbage in the pan, and then add hot water to just cover the vegetables. Sauté in the oven for 20 minutes. Meanwhile, peel the potatoes, cutting especially large ones in half. Lay them over the meat and continue to sauté until the meat and the vegetables are tender. Shortly before the process is done, heat the flour in a pan and mix it with the sour cream. Add this mixture to the roasting liquid to thicken. Sprinkle salt on the potatoes and continue to sauté for another 5 minutes. Sprinkle with chopped herbs before serving.

66

Chicken breasts in cream

8 chicken breasts,
1 1/2 glass sour cream,
2 tablespoons quince juice,
1 teaspoon chicken cubes,
1/2 teaspoon paprika,
salt, pepper,
1 clove garlic,
1 tablespoon spicy tomato sauce,
1 glass plus 3/4 glass dry bread crumbs,
1 glass melted butter

In deep dish mix sour cream with all of the ingredients except the dry bread crumbs. Place the chicken breasts into the mixture making sure that they are completely covered with sour cream. Marinate in the refrigerator for 12-24 hours. Remove the meat from the sour cream, leaving plenty of cream on the meat. Dredge in dry bread crumbs and arrange chicken in a shallow pan, so that the pieces do not touch each other. Pour half of the melted butter over the chicken breasts and put them in a medium oven for 30 minutes. Add the rest of the melted butter and bake for another 15 minutes. Serve with mashed or baked potatoes and fruit salad.

Roast lamb with garlic (8 servings)

1 kg (2 lb, 3 oz) boneless lamb,
1 tablespoon mustard,
5-6 cloves garlic,
400 g (14 oz) carrot,
1 teaspoon caraway seeds,
100 g (3.5 oz) butter, salt, pepper,
2 1/2 vegetable stock or water

Rub the lamb with the mustard. Place it in a dish and cover. Refrigerate for 2 days. Grind the caraway seeds in a spice grinder and chop the garlic. Rub the salt, pepper and ground caraway seeds over the lamb, and press garlic into the meat. Melt butter in a roasting pan. Lay slices of carrot on the bottom of the pan placing the meat on top. Bake in a hot oven until browned. Pour the vegetable stock or water over the meat. Reduce the temperature of the oven and continue to roast, occasionally basting with the roasting liquid. When the meat is done, slice and arrange lamb in a bowl. Add the cooked carrots, as well as baked potatoes (which you can bake along with the roast — boil the potatoes in their skins, let them cool, peel and place in the roasting pan when the roast is about half-done; sprinkle with salt and some of the roasting liquid).

White sauce

400 g (14 oz) chicken stock,
60 g (2.1 oz) butter,
1/2 leek or onion,
1/2 parsley root,
20 g (0.7 oz) flour, salt,
lemon juice, sugar,
dill or parsley

Finely dice the leek or onion, and parsley and sauté 40 g (1.4 oz) of butter. Add flour and stir constantly until heated through. Add the stock and salt and simmer for 10-15 minutes. Strain the liquid and press the vegetables through the sieve. Return to the pot along with dissolved lemon juice and sugar. Bring to a boil. Add the remaining butter and the chopped herbs.

67

Sautéed rabbit

1 kg (2 lb, 3 oz) rabbit meat, including the innards,
150 g (5.25 oz) smoked ham, 3 onions,
40 g (1.4 oz) butter,
1 tablespoon flour,
salt, pepper, bay leaf, paprika,
50 g (1.75 oz) dry red wine

Divide up the rabbit into 8-12 pieces. Remove the innards (the lungs, heart and liver). Remove the membrane from the liver. Wash the innards carefully and cut into small pieces. Melt butter in a large pan and brown the meat and innards. Cut the ham into small but thick pieces and slice the onions into rings. Add them to the meat and sauté, adding water as needed. When the meat is tender, add salt, spices and wine. Make a roux from the flour and butter and add it to the liquid to thicken. Sauté for another 10 minutes and sprinkle with chopped parsley or green onion. Serve with rice, dumplings or mashed potatoes.

Roast chicken

First version: Put 1 kg (2 lb, 3 oz) of sea salt in the bottom of a roasting pan and even it out. Dress the chicken, spread mustard over the breasts and lay it down on the salt. Roast for approximately 1 hour in a medium oven.

Second version: Rub a dry vegetable concentrate such as "Vegeta" all over the chicken and grill it.

Third version: Take a 1/2-liter bottle and fill it with warm water. Rub the chicken with salt, garlic and pepper and insert the bottle into its cavity so that bottle "sits" the chicken. Roast in the oven for 1 hour. Rub ketchup on the chicken before roasting in the oven.

Fourth version: Mix together 1/2 glass mayonnaise, 2 teaspoons salt, 2 chopped cloves of garlic and chopped dill, and rub the mixture over the chicken. Put the chicken in a paper bag or wrap it in foil. Roast for 1 hour.
Slice chicken into serving-sized pieces. Serve with baked potatoes, marinated fruit, baked apples stuffed with loganberry preserves, or a tomato and cucumber salad.

Sautéed chicken

1 chicken (1 kg (2 lb, 3 oz)),
40 g (1.4 oz) vegetable oil for frying

For the marinade:
1 onion, 1 clove garlic,
pepper, coriander, 4 cloves,
1-2 bay leaves,
ground ginger, sugar

Rinse the chicken. Chop the onion and garlic very finely and rub it over the chicken. Sprinkle with salt, sugar and spices. Wrap the chicken in cellophane (so that it does not dry out) and refrigerate for 10-12 hours. With a dry cloth, wipe off the spices from the chicken. Place in a large pot with the heated vegetable oil and roast in the oven until brown. Add enough water to cover half the chicken. Cover the pot or pan and sauté the chicken until it is ready. Slice into serving pieces and serve with baked potatoes, boiled carrots and cauliflower and white sauce (see below).

Chicken filet

2 chicken filets,
salt,
1 egg,
dry bread crumbs,
butter

Cut the chicken filets in half lengthwise, removing the skin. Tenderize with a meat mallet. Dip in beaten egg, then dredge in dry bread crumbs (mixed with salt). In a pan sauté chicken filets melted in butter until they are browned.

To stuff the chicken breasts:
150 g (5.25 oz) chicken meat,
35 g (1.225 oz) white bread soaked in milk,
1/4 glass milk,
1/4 glass sweet cream,
1 tablespoon butter

Grind chicken meat three times. Add the soaked bread and grind again. Whip the cream and slowly incorporate it (or 1 egg white) and the butter on to the meat. Salt to taste. Beat the mixture with an electric mixer until a small piece of it floats in water instead of sinking. Stuff the chicken filets with the mixture and prepare as directed above. Serve with baked potatoes, cabbage schnitzels, sautéed carrots or peas. Substitute turkey for chicken.

Roast goose with apples

1 goose (2-2.5 kg (4.3-5,5 lb)),
salt,
8-10 medium-tart apples,
water

Dress the goose, rub it with salt, and stuff with apples. (Put the apples in the goose whole or halved. Roast extra apples separately with the goose.) Sew up the goose and roast in a hot oven for 1-1 1/2 hours, basting frequently. Cut the goose in half lengthwise and then cut each half lengthwise again. Put the pieces in a large bowl and pour some of the roasting liquid over it. Serve with baked potatoes, sautéed sauerkraut or baked apples. Serve duck in the same way. Stuff goose with sautéed sauerkraut. Roast potatoes in the pan with the goose.

VEGETABLE AND MUSHROOM DISHES

Mushroom sauce

150 g (5.25 oz) water or vegetable stock,
50 g (1.75 oz) sour cream,
100 g (3.5 oz) mushrooms (regular mush-
  rooms, chanterelles, etc.),
30 g (1.05 oz) butter,
30 g (1.05 oz) onion,
10 g (0.35 oz) flour,
salt, pepper

Chop the onions and sauté them for a bit in the butter. Slice the mushrooms and add them to the pan. Sauté until tender. Add the flour, stir to heat through, add the vegetable stock or water and bring to a boil. Add sour cream, salt and pepper and simmer for 10-15 minutes.

Prepare this sauce with dried mushrooms (10 g). Rinse and blanch mushrooms with boiling water, pour cold water over them and allow to soak for 3-4 hours. Cook them in the soaking water. Slice the mushrooms and sauté with chopped onion. Make a sauce with the cooking liquid.

Boiled potatoes (Latvian style)

500 g (17.5 oz) potato,
salt, dill or parsley

Rinse and peel the potatoes and then rinse them again. If the potatoes are of different sizes, cut up the larger ones. Put the potatoes in boiling water, add salt and boil for 25-30 minutes. When the potatoes are almost tender, drain off the water, cover the pot and put it on a low flame for several minutes. Remove the lid, let the potatoes dry and shake the pot. This will make the potatoes starchy and tasty. Put the potatoes in a deep bowl and sprinkle with dill or parsley. Latvians serve boiled potatoes with all kinds of dishes, including cottage cheese and herring, mushrooms and sour cream, and bacon, mushroom, tomato and other sauces.

Rolled cabbage

1 head of cabbage, salt to taste, dill

Separate the large leaves of a cabbage and boil in salted water. When they are tender, roll them up, brush them with melted butter and sprinkle them with chopped dill. Serve with various meat and fish dishes.

Mashed grated potatoes

First version:
800 g (28 oz) potato,
300 g (10.5 oz) smoked bacon, 1-2 onions

Peel and grate potatoes on a vegetable grater. Cut 50 g (1.75 oz) of the smoked bacon into small pieces and chop the onions. Put the bacon and onions in a deep pan and sauté. Add potatoes and salt, and bake in the oven until a brown crust forms on the top of the potatoes. Keep the pan covered for the first 20 minutes, then bake uncovered. Serve with loganberry preserves or sour cream.

Second version:
450 g (15.75 oz) potato,
80 g (2.8 oz) mild white cheese,
1-2 eggs,
150 g (5.25 oz) milk,
salt, pepper, fat

Peel and grate potatoes on a vegetable grater. Grate cheese and beat the eggs with milk, salt and pepper. Mix all of the ingredients together. Pour it into a greased loaf pan and bake in a medium oven for approximately 40 minutes. Serve with sour cream or loganberry preserves.

Third version:
450 g (15.75 oz) potato, salt,
butter or vegetable oil

Peel and grate potatoes. Add salt. Grease a roasting pan or rub it with the vegetable oil. Spoon mounds of potato into the pan, pressing down to smooth them into pancakes. Bake in the

oven until the pancakes are light brown. Serve with loganberry preserves or sour cream. Serve the pancakes cold, putting a piece of herring filet, pickle and/or sprat on top of each one.

Potato roll

500 g (17.5 oz) potato,
1 egg, salt,
10 g (0.35 oz) sour cream,
5 g (0.175 oz) mild white cheese (grated),
20 g (0.7 oz) vegetable oil for frying

For the filling:
200 g (7 oz) cooked beef,
30 g (1.05 oz) onion,
30 g (1.05 oz) butter,
pepper, beef stock

Boil potatoes in salted water. Drain, dry and mash them (or run them through a meat grinder). Add the egg and mix well. Wet a piece of cheesecloth and spread the potatoes over the cloth at a thickness of 1 cm (0.4 inches). Spread the meat filling over the potatoes and then roll up the potato, using the cheesecloth to help you. Remove the cloth before cooking the roll. Heat the vegetable oil in a roasting pan. Place the roll in the pan, spread with sour cream and sprinkle with grated cheese. Bake in the oven until brown.

For the filling: Cut up the onion and sauté it in butter. Grind the cooked beef and add it to the pan with a little beef stock, salt and pepper. Heat through.

Slice the potato roll. Arrange the slices in a shallow dish and serve with sour cream and a vegetable salad.

Potato patties

>*400 g (14 oz) potatoes,*
>*30 g (1.05 oz) onion,*
>*20 g (0.7 oz) butter,*
>*20 g (0.7 oz) flour,*
>*1 egg, salt,*
>*bread crumbs,*
>*vegetable oil*

Boil the potatoes in salted water. Drain, dry and mash them. Cool them a bit (to 40-50°C or 104-122°F). Chop the onion and sauté it in some butter. Add onion, egg, flour and salt to the mashed potatoes and mix thoroughly. Shape into round patties. Dredge in bread crumbs and brown in hot pan with oil. Arrange the patties in a shallow dish and serve with sour cream, mushroom, tomato or other sauce, as well as a vegetable salad.

Oven-baked potatoes

>*500 g (17.5 oz) potato*

Wash and scrub medium-sized potatoes until they are clean. Put them dry. Place potatoes on a rack in a hot oven and bake them until the skin is dry. Put the potatoes in a sieve and shake it so that the skin begin to separate from the potatoes. Return to the oven until the potatoes are tender. Traditionally Latvians have also baked potatoes in hot ashes, first rinsing and drying them and then putting in the hot ashes in the hearth and piling red-hot coals on top of them. Serve with cottage cheese, butter and buttermilk or sour milk.

Cabbage schnitzel

>First version:
>*500 g (17.5 oz) cabbage,*
>*1 egg,*
>*30 g (1.05 oz) bread crumbs,*
>*1 teaspoon chopped dill,*
>*vegetable oil for frying*

Cut a firm, medium-sized head of cabbage in half, place in boiling salted water and boil until tender, but still firm. Remove the cabbage from the water. Let it cool and cut into slices 1 cm (0.4 inches) thick. (Each slice should include part of the heart of the cabbage so that the leaves hold together.) Beat the egg and mix it with the dill. Dip the cabbage pieces into the egg and dredge in dry bread crumbs. Brown in oil on both sides. Put cooled cabbage slices to roast in the oven until they are brown.

>Second version:
>*500 g (17.5 oz) cabbage,*
>*salt, flour, vegetable oil*

>For the batter:
>*1-1 1/2 eggs,*
>*1-1 1/2 tablespoon milk,*
>*1-1 1/2 tablespoon flour,*
>*1/2 tablespoon chopped dill, salt*

Mix all of the ingredients for the batter thoroughly. Boil cabbage leaves in salted water until tender and drain. Fold or roll each leaf as though you were making rolled cabbage. Dredge the rolls in flour, dip them in the batter and deep fry until light brown.

Cabbage schnitzel is served with various meat, fowl and fish dishes.

Bacon sauce

> 25 g (0.875 oz) bacon,
> 25 g (0.875 oz) onion,
> 1 glass beef stock,
> 10 g (0.35 oz) flour,
> 1 bay leaf,
> 1 clove,
> 1/2 tablespoon vinegar,
> salt,
> 1/2 teaspoon sugar,
> sour cream

Cut the bacon into small pieces and chop the onion. Sauté in a pan. Add the flour and heat it through. Add the beef stock and vinegar. Simmer over a low flame for 4-8 minutes. Add all of the other ingredients, except the sour cream. Simmer for another 10 minutes. Strain, add the sour cream and bring back to a boil.

Sautéed carrots and peas

> 300 g (10.5 oz) carrots,
> 30 g (1.05 oz) butter,
> 100 g (3.5 oz) preserved peas (without the liquid),
> salt, sugar, water

Dice the carrots. Boil in salted water. Adding a pinch of sugar to the butter, sauté the carrots in a pan until they are tender and the water has evaporated. Add the peas and heat through, stirring. Serve the sauté as an accompaniment to chicken, meat and fish dishes.

Tomato sauce

> 150 g (5.25 oz) beef stock,
> 20 g (0.7 oz) butter,
> 20 g (0.7 oz) onion,
> 120 g (4.2 oz) parsley and celery,
> 50 g (1.75 oz) tomato purée,
> 10 g (0.35 oz) flour,
> 50 g (1.75 oz) sour cream,
> salt, sugar, pepper, bay leaves

Sprinkle flour in a pan with butter and heat through. Add the stock and simmer for 10 minutes. Slice the onions, celery and parsley and sauté them in separate pan with butter. Add vegetables tomato purée, salt, sugar, pepper and bay leaves to the pot, and simmer for 15 minutes. Strain the sauce. Press the vegetables through a sieve and return to the pot. Add sour cream and bring to a boil.

Carrot dumplings

> 250 g (8.75 oz) carrot,
> 1 egg,
> 1/4 glass milk,
> 1 teaspoon melted butter,
> 100-150 g (3.5-5.25 oz) flour,
> salt, sugar

Finely grate the carrots. Add egg, salt, sugar, melted butter and flour. Gradually add milk, stirring all the while. Drop the mixture into boiling vegetable stock, teaspoon by teaspoon, cook until tender. Serve with sour cream.

Stuffed cabbage rolls (Latvian style)

500 g (17.5 oz) cabbage,
vegetable oil for frying,
flour,
salt,
1/3 glass sour cream,
vegetable stock

First version:
For the vegetable stuffing:
100 g (3.5 oz) carrot,
40 g (1.4 oz) onion,
50 g (1.75 oz) cooked rice,
1 teaspoon tomato purée,
salt, pepper,
vegetable oil

Choose a medium-sized (and not too firm) head of cabbage. Cut out the core. Place the cabbage in salted water and boil until the leaves are flexible. Remove from the water and peel off individual leaves. Use a meat mallet to tenderize the center rib of each leaf. Place the stuffing at the base of each leaf, fold over the edges and roll it up. Dredge the rolls in flour and sauté in vegetable oil until they are light brown. Put the rolls in a pan, in one or two layers. Add the vegetable stock and sour cream. Cover the pan and bake in the oven until ready.

For the filling: Grate the carrots and chop the onion. Sauté them in vegetable oil. Add the tomato purée, salt and pepper, and a little of water, and sauté for 10-15 minutes. Add the cooked rise and stir.

Second version:
Stuff the cabbage leaves with meat

stuffing:
250 g (8.75 oz) ground pork,
35 g cooked rice,
1 small onion,
salt, pepper

Chop the onion and sauté in butter. Mix it together with all of the other ingredients and proceed as in the first version.

Sautéed sauerkraut

400 g (14 oz) sauerkraut,
water,
50 g (1.75 oz) carrot,
30 g (1.05 oz) onion,
50 g (1.75 oz) butter,
salt, sugar to taste

Melt butter in a large pot. Chop the onion and sauté it in the butter until it is light brown. Chop the sauerkraut into smaller pieces and add it to the pot. If you want the sautéed sauerkraut to be light in color, cover the sautéing onions with boiling water. Immediately cover the pot and leave to cook over a low flame. If you want the sauerkraut to be darker in color, sauté the onions in the uncovered pan adding water after some time. Sauté the sauerkraut for 2-3 hours. In the last 20 minutes, grate the carrots and add those to the pot. When it is tender, add salt and sugar. (If the sauerkraut is not as dark as you would like, caramelize some sugar and add it to the pot.) Sautéed sauerkraut is served with roast pork, pork chops and other fatty meat dishes.

Sautéed sweet-and-sour cabbage

> *500 g (17.5 oz) cabbage,*
> *50 g (1.75 oz) butter,*
> *100-150 g (3.5-5.25 oz) tart apples,*
> *salt, sugar, dill*

Slice the cabbage into thin slivers. Place into a clay or casserole dish. Sprinkle with 1/2 teaspoon salt. Press cabbage with a potato masher until the cabbage yields its juice. Transfer all of the contents of the bowl, including the juice, to a pot and sauté. Slice the apple. When the juice of the cabbage begins to evaporate, add the butter, the sliced apple and sugar. Continue to sauté. When the cabbage and apples are tender, add the chopped dill. You may also add slices of hard-boiled egg and then use the mixture to stuff *pīrāgi*. Sweet-and-sour cabbage is traditionally served with pork and lamb.

Cabbage patties

> *500 g (17.5 oz) cabbage,*
> *1/4 glass manna-croup,*
> *1 onion, 1 egg,*
> *10 g butter, salt,*
> *bread crumbs,*
> *vegetable oil*

Grate the cabbage and press with a potato masher until the juice separates. Sauté the cabbage mixture until the juice evaporates. Add the manna-croup, stir and heat for 15-20 minutes, until the mixture starts to separate from the pot. Cool. Chop the onion and brown in butter. Add the onion, salt and egg to the cabbage mixture and stir well. Shape into small patties. Dredge in bread crumbs, and sauté in oil until they are light brown. Serve the patties with sour cream or tomato sauce.

Cauliflower with burnt butter and bread crumbs

> *700 g (24.5 oz) cauliflower,*
> *50 g (1.75 oz) butter,*
> *10 g bread crumbs,*
> *1/3 lemon or lemon juice*

Choose firm, medium-sized heads of cauliflower. Soak them in vinegar water (1 tablespoon of vinegar per 1 l (1 quart + 4 tablespoons) of water) for 15-20 minutes. Rinse the cauliflower. Place in boiling salted water and boil until tender. Remove the cauliflower from the water with a slotted spoon and place in a shallow dish. Pour burnt butter on top of the cauliflower. Add bread crumbs (mixed with lemon juice or dissolved lemon juice).

Beets in cream

> *400 g (14 oz) cooked beets,*
> *1 teaspoon butter,*
> *50 g (1.75 oz) sour cream,*
> *salt, sugar, lemon juice*

Peel and coarsely grate cooked beets. Sauté in a pot with butter and heat through, stirring all the while. Add sour cream, salt, sugar and lemon juice. Serve with boiled potatoes or as an accompaniment to meat dishes.

Breaded cauliflower

400 g (14 oz) cauliflower,
salt,
vegetable oil.

For the dough:
80 g (2.8 oz) milk,
60 g (2.1 oz) flour,
2 eggs, salt

Break the cauliflower into individual pieces, rinse, and boil in salted water until they are almost tender. Remove the pieces from the pot and drain them in a sieve. Dip each piece into the dough and deep fry it. Decorate the cauliflower with dill or parsley and lemon slices. Drizzle with melted butter and serve with mashed potatoes.

For the dough: Beat the egg yolks with salt and add milk. Pour the liquid into the flour and mix until you get a uniform dough. Set aside for 10-20 minutes. Before frying, whip the egg whites until foamy and fold into the dough.

Vegetable casserole

200 g (7 oz) cabbage,
150 g (5.25 oz) carrot,
100 g (3.5 oz) preserved peas,
1 parsley root,
1 stalk celery,
1 small onion,
50 g (1.75 oz) butter,
20 g (0.7 oz) manna-croup,
salt, chopped dill or parsley, 1 egg,
60 g (2.1 oz) milk or sweet cream,
10 g (0.35 oz) mild white cheese

Chop the onion, parsley and celery finely and sauté them in butter. Coursely grate the carrots and add them to the pan. Sauté adding a little water. Continue to cook for 10-15 minutes. Add sliced cabbage and the peas to the pan. Sauté until all of the vegetables are nearly tender. Add manna-croup and stir well. Remove the pan from the flame and let the vegetables cool. Beat the egg with the milk or cream, as well as the chopped dill or parsley. Pour the egg mixture over the vegetables. Sprinkle bread crumbs into a greased casserole dish. Pour the mixture into dish. Top it with the grated cheese and bake in the oven. Serve the casserole with melted butter or a bread crumb sauce.

Carrot and cottage cheese casserole

300 g (10.5 oz) carrot,
50 g (1.75 oz) butter,
100 g (3.5 oz) dry cottage cheese,
2 eggs,
1 teaspoon sugar,
salt,
bread crumbs

Finely grate carrots. Add a little water, butter, salt and sugar to a pan, and sauté the carrots until they are tender. (All of the water should evaporate.) Press the cottage cheese through a sieve. Separate the eggs. Mix the cottage cheese and egg yolks with the carrots. Beat the egg whites until they are foamy and fold them into the carrots. Sprinkle a greased, ovenproof dish with bread crumbs. Pour the carrot mixture into the dish, sprinkle remaining bread crumbs over the top and bake in the oven until done. Serve with sour cream or loganberry preserves.

Vegetable bowl

500 g (17.5 oz) cabbage,
200 g (7 oz) carrots,
1/2 glass preserved peas, salt,
40 g (1.4 oz) butter

Cut the cabbage in half. Put the cabbage and whole carrots in boiling salted water. When the vegetables are tender, remove them from the pot with a slotted spoon and drain. Slice the cabbage and carrot and place them in a warm bowl. Warm the peas separately (on the stove or in a microwave) and add them to the bowl. Drizzle with melted butter. Serve with boiled rutabagas. The vegetable bowl is served as an accompaniment to various meat dishes: roasts, rolled meats and sausages.

Rutabaga patties

500 g (17.5 oz) rutabaga,
100 g (3.5 oz) bread crumbs,
1-2 eggs,
1 tablespoon cream cheese,
salt, vegetable oil

Peel and quarter rutabagas. Boil for 5 minutes. Drain the water from the pot and pour boiling salted water over the rutabagas. Boil until they are tender. Allow the rutabagas to cool. Grind them through a meat grinder or a food processor. Add bread crumbs, eggs, cream cheese (heated) and salt. Shape into small patties. Dredge them in bread crumbs and sauté in vegetable oil until browned. Serve with mushroom or bacon sauce.

Rutabaga casserole

500 g (17.5 oz) rutabaga,
2 eggs,
50 g (1.75 oz) butter,
1 tablespoon sour cream,
1 tablespoon honey,
1 tablespoon bread crumbs,
salt

Peel the rutabagas and cut them into pieces. Blanch in boiling water. Remove the pot from the flame and let the water cool. Transfer the rutabagas to boiling salted water. Cook until tender. Grind rutabagas through a meat grinder or a food processor. Separate the eggs. Whip the egg whites until they are foamy, adding a touch of salt. Add egg yolks, bread crumbs, sour cream and egg whites to the rutabagas. Add honey and melted butter, blending well. Place the rutabaga mixture into a greased casserole dish. Sprinkle bread crumbs on top, and drizzle with honey butter. Bake in the oven for 20-25 minutes. Serve with grilled sandwiches or as an accompaniment to chicken dishes.

Bread crumb sauce

30 g (1.05 oz) bread crumbs,
110 g (3.85 oz) butter,
pinch lemon juice

Melt the butter and sauté the bread crumbs until they are golden. Dissolve the lemon juice in a little water and add it to the pan. Mix well.

Stuffed rutabaga

First version:
400 g (14 oz) rutabaga,
200 g (7 oz) sour cream sauce,
20 g (0.7 oz) cheese

For the stuffing:
150 g (5.25 oz) pork,
1 onion,
1 tablespoon cooked rice,
salt, pepper

Choose medium-sized rutabagas. Boil whole rutabagas until they are almost tender. Peel the rutabagas and cut off their tops. Do not discard. Scoop out the insides, leaving 1 to 1 1/2 centimeters of flesh. Pour the stuffing into the rutabagas. Replace the tops, and arrange them in a deep pan in one layer. Pour the sour cream sauce over them. Sprinkle with grated cheese and and bake in the oven until ready. For the stuffing, simply grind the pork and mix together with the other ingredients.

Sour cream sauce

100 g (3.5 oz) water,
vegetable or beef stock,
100 g (3.5 oz) sour cream,
10 g (0.35 oz) butter,
10 g (0.35 oz) flour,
salt, spices

Heat the flour in a pan, add butter and mix well. Add water, vegetable or beef stock, stir well and simmer for 10-15 minutes. Add sour cream, salt and pepper and simmer for another

10 minutes. Add sautéed onion, spicy tomato sauce (20 g (0.7 oz), or sautéed vegetables (onions, carrots, parsley or celery) for the last 10-15 minutes. Serve with horseradish. Sprinkle with chopped dill or parsley.

Second version:
400 g (14 oz) rutabaga,
200 g (7 oz) tomato purée

For the stuffing:
250 g (8.75 oz) mushrooms,
50 g (1.75 oz) smoked bacon,
1 onion

Dice the mushrooms. Sauté them in their own juice. Slice the bacon. Chop onion and sauté them in butter until they are translucent. Mix all of the ingredients, salt to taste and stuff the rutabagas as instructed above.

Sautéed beets and bacon

400 g (14 oz) grated,
cooked beets,
100 g (3.5 oz) smoked bacon,
30 g (1.05 oz) onion,
6 g (0.2 oz) flour,
salt, horseradish root,
sour cream

Sauté sliced bacon and onion in a pan. Add grated beets in a separate pan. Heat flour. Sprinkle over the vegetables and stir. Add a little boiling water with salt. Grate the horseradish and add it to the pan. Sauté for 5-8 minutes. Add 1 tablespoon of sour cream and heat through.

Warm beet and bacon snacks with cottage cheese

200 g (7 oz) cooked beets,
50 g (1.75 oz) smoked bacon, 1 onion,
50-75 g (1.75-2.625 oz) dry cottage cheese,
1 tablespoon sour cream,
salt, lemon juice

Peel and slice the beets. Dice the bacon and chop the onion. Sauté in butter. Add the beets, salt and lemon juice to taste. Heat through. Add cottage cheese and sour cream and mix well. Serve with boiled potatoes and *kefir*, or yogurt.

Pumpkin and cottage cheese casserole

250 g (8.75 oz) pumpkin,
250 g (8.75 oz) dry cottage cheese,
1 medium-tart apple, 2 eggs,
1/4-1/3 glass sugar,
50 g (1.75 oz) butter,
the zest of 1 lemon,
dry bread crumbs,
flour

Peel and slice the pumpkin. Dredge the slices in flour and brown them in butter. Separate the eggs. Beat the yolks with half of the sugar and add to the cottage cheese. Grate the onion. Peel and dice the apple. Mix with cottage cheese. Pour remaining butter from the pan over mixture. Grease a casserole dish and sprinkle the inside with bread crumbs. Layer pumpkin slices and cottage cheese in the dish, sprinkling bread crumbs top layer. Bake in a medium oven for 20 minutes. Whip the egg whites with the remaining sugar and pour on top of the casserole. Continue to bake until the top starts to yellow. Serve with fruit sauce.

Fried pumpkin

First version:
500 g (17.5 oz) pumpkin,
salt,
lemon juice, 1 egg,
1 tablespoon dry bread crumbs,
1 tablespoon flour,
30 g (1.05 oz) butter

Peel the pumpkin. Cut into slices that are 1/2 cm (0.2 inches) thick. Sprinkle with salt and a little lemon juice dissolved in water. Set aside for 10-15 minutes. Beat the egg. Dip each slice of pumpkin in the egg and dredge in bread crumbs. Fry in melted butter turning the pumpkin until it is tender and browned. Serve with loganberry preserves.

Second version:
500 g (17.5 oz) pumpkin, salt,
mixture of flour and bread crumbs,
vegetable oil

Peel the pumpkin. Cut into slices that are 1/2 cm (0.2 inches) thick. Sprinkle generously with salt. Set aside for 1 hour. Dredge each slice in the mixture of flour and bread crumbs and fry in vegetable oil until browned. Serve with mashed potatoes and bacon or mushroom sauce.

Pumpkin and apple casserole

250 g (8.75 oz) pumpkin,
250 g (8.75 oz) medium-tart apple,
1/2 glass milk,
25-50 (0.875-1.75 oz) sugar,
1 egg,
1 tablespoon mann-croup,
50 g (1.75 oz) butter,
cinnamon,
bread crumbs

Peel and coarsely grate the pumpkin. Sauté in 1 tablespoon of butter until almost tender. Peel and grate the apples. Add them to the pan and sauté for another 10 minutes. Cool the mixture. Put the manna-croup in the milk and allow it to absorb the liquid. Separate the egg. Beat the egg yolk with one half of the sugar. Add it to the milk mixture, adding cinnamon to taste. Pour the mixture into the pan with the pumpkin and apple. Whip the egg white with the remaining sugar and pour on to pan. Distribute the mixture into individual little forms, dot with butter and bake in the oven for approximately 30 minutes.

Fried onions

300 g (10.5 oz) onion,
2 tablespoons flour,
1-2 tablespoons sugar,
1-2 glasses milk,
salt,
paprika,
vegetable oil

Choose onions of equal size. Peel and slice into thin (3 mm thick) slices. Arrange them in a shallow dish. Pour the milk over them and let stand in the refrigerator for 20 minutes. Roll each slice in flour, sprinkle with sugar and cook over a high flame. Add salt and paprika over the slices before serving. Serve with roasts and/or wild game. Separate onions into rings and prepared as above. Onion rings can be used to decorate meat dishes.

Mushroom patties

300 g (10.5 oz) cooked or salted mushrooms,
50 g (1.75 oz) white bread soaked in 50 g (1.75 oz) milk,
30 g (1.05 oz) onion,
20 g (0.7 oz) butter,
1 egg,
salt, pepper,
bread crumbs

Grind mushrooms with the soaked bread. Chop the onion and sauté in butter. Beat the egg. Add the onion, egg, salt and pepper to the mushroom mixture and stir well. Shape the mixture into small patties, dredge them in the bread crumbs and fry them in the melted butter until they are browned on both sides. Optional second step: Put the patties in a deep dish, pour sour cream over them and bake for another 5-6 minutes in the oven. Serve the patties with boiled potatoes, mashed potatoes, sour cream sauce and pickles.

Fried chanterelles

First version:
400 g (14 oz) fresh chanterelles,
50 g (1.75 oz) butter,
30 g (1.05 oz) onion,
salt

Rinse mushrooms well and slice. Chop the onion and sauté in butter. Add the mushrooms and salt and sauté for 10-15 minutes, stirring. Add a little sour cream to the mixture and serve.

Second version:
400 g (14 oz) fresh chanterelles,
1 egg,
10 g (0.35 oz) flour,
20 g (0.7 oz) bread crumbs,
salt, pepper,
50 g (1.75 oz) vegetable oil

Choose firm, medium-sized chanterelles. Clean them, cut off their stems, and slice 1/2 cm (0.2 inches) thick. Sprinkle salt and pepper on the mushrooms. Dredge in flour. Dip mushrooms in beaten egg and roll in bread crumbs. Sauté in vegetable oil until browned on both sides. Serve with baked potatoes, vegetable salad or as an accompaniment to meat or fish dishes.

Sautéed mushrooms

300 g (10.5 oz) cooked or salted mushrooms,
100 g (3.5 oz) smoked bacon,
30 g (1.05 oz) onion,
6 g (0.2 oz) flour,
100 g (3.5 oz) water,
30 g (1.05 oz) sour cream

Dice the bacon and chop the onion. Sauté in butter. Chop mushrooms and add them to the pan. Sauté while stirring. Sprinkle with flour, add water and salt and mix well. Sauté for 10-15 minutes. Add the sour cream. Sautéed mushrooms can be served with boiled potatoes and pickles.

LEGUMES

Traditional Latvian peas with bacon

200 g (7 oz) gray peas,
60 g (2.1 oz) cured bacon,
40 g (1.4 oz) onion,
salt

Soak the peas thoroughly and drain. Put them in a pot with water to cover and boil until tender. Chop the onion and the cured bacon well. Sauté onions and bacon in a separate pan. Serve the peas in clay bowls (if possible), pouring the bacon and onion mixture over each serving. Serve with buttermilk. Use fresh bacon instead of cured.

Peas with bacon sauce

240 g (8.4 oz) yellow or gray peas,
salt

For the sauce:
60 g (2.1 oz) cured bacon,
40 g (1.4 oz) onion,
10 g (0.35 oz) flour,
1 glass water,
40 g (1.4 oz) sour cream,
salt,
chopped herbs

Soak the peas thoroughly and boil in salted water until they are tender. Chop the onion and bacon and sauté in butter. Add flour to the pan, mix well, and allow the flour to brown. Add water, stir, and cook for 10 minutes. Add the sour cream and salt. Put the peas in a deep dish and smother them with the bacon sauce, sprinkling chopped herbs on top. Use beans instead of peas.

Bean patties

200 g (7 oz) beans,
40 g (1.4 oz) white bread soaked in milk,
1 egg,
40 g (1.4 oz) sour cream,
6 g (0.2 oz) caraway seeds,
salt,
bread crumbs,
butter

Soak the beans and then boil them until they are tender. Remove the bread from the milk and squeeze out most of the liquid. Grind the beans together with the bread. Lightly toast the caraway seeds . Add caraway along with the egg, sour cream and salt to the mixture. Stir well. Make patties from the mixture, dredge them in bread crumbs and in a greased castiron pan brown on both sides. Serve with cream or to-mato sauce. Make the patties with 50 g (1.75 oz) of beans and 50 g (1.75 oz) of cottage cheese.

Yellow bean with butter

800 g (28 oz) yellow beans,
salt, 100 g (3.5 oz) butter,
1 tablespoon bread crumbs

Choose young and tender yellow beans for this dish. Cut off both ends of the pods and remove the vein on either side of the pod. Rinse the pods and put them in boiling salt water until they are tender. Remove them from the water with a slotted spoon and arrange in a shallow dish. Brown butter. Mix together with bread crumbs and pour it over the beans.

Oven-baked peas

240 g (8.4 oz) gray peas, salt

Soak the peas thoroughly and boil in salted water until they are almost tender. Drain. Pour the peas into a greased casserole dish. Heat in the oven, stirring occasionally, until they are dry and nicely brown. Serve with beer or buttermilk.

Pea dumplings

200 g (7 oz) gray peas,
100 g (3.5 oz) potato,
60 g (2.1 oz) cured bacon,
30 g (1.05 oz) onion,
50 g (1.75 oz) hemp butter (if available)

Soak the peas thoroughly. Peel the potatoes. Boil peas and potatoes separately until they are tender. Drain and grind ingredients twice. Chop the onion and bacon and sauté them in butter. Add to the pea mixture, along with the hemp butter and the salt. Mix well. Shape the mixture into small dumplings and arrange them in a shallow dish. Serve with milk or buttermilk.

Mixed beans

2 kg beans, salt

Choose a variety of beans in which the beans are smaller and the pods are thinner. Rinse the beans and boil for 30 minutes. Add salt to taste and continue to cook until the beans are tender. Drain the beans and serve them with sour porridge or buttermilk. Split open the pods to get at the beans or remove the beans from the pods before serving. Serve with bacon sauce.

Mashed peas

240 g (8.4 oz) peas,
40 g (1.4 oz) butter,
20 g (0.7 oz) onion,
1 glass milk,
40 g (1.4 oz) sour cream, salt

Soak the peas, boil in salted water until they are tender. Drain and grind peas. Chop the onion and sauté in butter in a pot. Add the ground peas in a separate pot. Heat the milk to boiling. Add it to the peas. Salt to taste. Heat through, and add sour cream (optional). Serve the peas with cooked bacon, melted butter or bacon sauce.

PORRIDGES
AND
MACARONI DISHES

Koča

> *150 g (5.25 oz) pearl-barley,*
> *70 g (2.45 oz) smoked bacon,*
> *50 g (1.75 oz) onion,*
> *600 g (21 oz) water,*
> *salt*

Soak the pearl-barley for 5-6 hours in cold water. Toast in the oven until it is light yellow. Dice the bacon and chop the onion, and sauté in butter. Layer the barley and bacon-onion mixture in a casserole dish and add hot water to cover. Salt to taste and cook until the barley is plump. Tightly cover the dish and bake in the oven for 2 hours. Serve with buttermilk or sour milk.

Barley porridge

> *150 barley grouts,*
> *300 g (10.5 oz) water,*
> *200 g (7 oz) milk,*
> *30 g (1.05 oz) butter or bacon,*
> *salt*

Rinse the barley grouts and boil them in salt water until they are almost tender. Heat the milk in a separate pot and add it to the barley. Bake in the oven until the barley is tender. Serve with fried bacon and milk.

Barley and potato porridge

> *80 g (2.8 oz) barley grouts,*
> *300 g (10.5 oz) potato,*
> *200 g (7 oz) water,*
> *200 g (7 oz) milk,*
> *80 g (2.8 oz) smoked bacon,*
> *50 g (1.75 oz) onion,*
> *salt*

Rinse the grouts and boil them in water until they are almost tender. Peel and slice the potatoes and add them to the pot, along with salt to taste. Boil until the potatoes are almost tender. Heat the milk separately to boiling and add it to the pot. Cook and stir until the grouts are completely tender. Serve with fried bacon and onion and a glass of milk. Substitute finely diced carrots, rutabaga or cabbage for the potatoes if you like.

Barley and pea porridge

80 g (2.8 oz) barley grouts,
80 g (2.8 oz) peas,
300 g (10.5 oz) water,
300 g (10.5 oz) milk,
80 g (2.8 oz) smoked bacon,
50 g (1.75 oz) onion,
salt

Soak the peas and boil them until they are tender. Rinse the barley and add to the pot. Allow them to plump up. Add salt to taste. Heat milk to boiling and add it to the pot. Continue cooking until the barley is tender and the peas are falling apart. Serve with fried bacon and onions, and with sour milk, *kefir*, or buttermilk.

Tart oatmeal porridge

270 g oats (not instant),
750 g (26.25 oz) water,
1 slice rye bread,
salt

Put the oats in a clay jug (glass will do) and add warm water to cover. Put in the rye bread, cover with a cloth and set aside in a warm place for 1-2 days to allow the porridge to mixture sour. Press all of the solids through a fine mesh sieve or a piece of cheesecloth. What remains in the sieve or the cloth are the husks of the oats and the crusts of the bread. Add another 2 cups of water to the liquid which you have squeezed out. Pour the liquid into a pot. Salt to taste and heat, stirring all the while, to a boil. If the porridge is too thick or lumpy, add a bit of hot water. Serve the porridge in small clay bowls (if you have them), adding melted butter to hot porridge, or milk to cold porridge.

Baked macaroni and bacon

160 g (5.6 oz) pasta of your choice,
1 l (1 quart + 4 tablespoons) water,
salt,
50 g (1.75 oz) smoked bacon,
20 g (0.7 oz) onion,
1 egg,
100 g (3.5 oz) milk,
bread crumbs

Boil pasta in salt water and drain. Cut the bacon and chop the onion, and sauté. Add the bacon and onions to the boiled pasta, stir ring thoroughly. Pour the mixture into a greased casserole dish sprinkled with bread crumbs. Mix together the egg and milk and pour over the casserole. Sprinkle more bread crumbs on top. Bake in the oven for 20-25 minutes. Serve with sour cream and vegetable salad.

Rye porridge

400 g (14 oz) coarse rye flour,
1 l (1 quart + 4 tablespoons) water,
salt

Boil water and salt, stir in the flour and heat for 5 minutes, stirring with a wooden spoon, until the porridge is ready. Serve with bacon, along with buttermilk or milk. Make porridge with coarse wheat or barley flour.

85

Macaroni and cottage cheese casserole

100 g (3.5 oz) pasta,
water,
salt,
150 g (5.25 oz) dry cottage cheese,
30 g (1.05 oz) butter,
40 g (1.4 oz) sugar,
1 egg,
bread crumbs

Boil the pasta in salt water and drain. Allow to cool. Separate the egg. Beat together the egg yolk, milk and sugar. Process or grind the cottage cheese and add it, along with the pasta, to the milk mixture. Whip the egg white until it is foamy and fold into the mixture. Pour the mixture into a greased casserole dish sprinkled with bread crumbs. Sprinkle bread crumbs on top and bake in the oven until the casserole is nicely browned and is pulling away from the sides of the pan. Invert the casserole dish onto a plate, remove the casserole and serve it with butter or sour cream.

COTTAGE CHEESE DISHES

Cottage cheese with whipped cream

First version:
200 g (7 oz) dry cottage cheese,
50 g (1.75 oz) sugar,
100 g (3.5 oz) sweet cream,
vanilla sugar or grated zest of 1 lemon,
fruit

Process or grind the cottage cheese two or three times. Add the sugar and lemon zest and whip until the sugar has dissolved. Whip the cream and fold into the mixture. Serve with fruit or berries.

Second version:
200 g (7 oz) dry cottage cheese,
40 g (1.4 oz) sugar,
salt,
1 egg yolk,
20 g (0.7 oz) butter,
100 g (3.5 oz) sweet cream,
vanilla sugar,
20 g (0.7 oz) chocolate

Whip the egg yolk with the sugar and the vanilla sugar. Process or grind the cottage cheese and add it to the mixture along with half of the sweet cream and a bit of salt. Melt the butter in a pot, add the cottage cheese mixture and heat just to boiling. (Do not allow the mixture to boil.) Remove from the flame and stir to cool. Refrigerate for 1-2 hours. Before serving, remove the mixture from the dish and decorate it with whipped cream and grated chocolate.

Cottage cheese dumplings

300 g (10.5 oz) dry cottage cheese,
2 eggs,
30 g (1.05 oz) flour,
10 g manna-croup,
20 g (0.7 oz) sour cream,
sugar,
salt,
caraway seeds,
butter

Mix together all of the ingredients except for the sour cream. With wet fingers shape the mixture into dumplings. Boil in salted water until they are heated through and rise to the top of the pot. Remove dumplings from the pot with a slotted spoon. Arrange them in a dish and drizzle with melted butter (to keep them from sticking together), and serve with sour cream.

Sweet cottage cheese casserole

240 g (8.4 oz) dry cottage cheese,
30-40 g sugar, 2 eggs,
30 g (1.05 oz) butter,
grated zest of 1 lemon or vanilla sugar,
salt,
20 g (0.7 oz) flour,
10 g manna-croup,
30 g (1.05 oz) raisins,
bread crumbs

Separate the eggs. Beat together the butter, sugar, egg yolks and lemon zest or vanilla sugar. Process or grind the cottage cheese and add it to the mixture. Salt to taste. Rinse and dry the raisins. Toss them with some flour and add them to the mixture. Mix well. Beat the egg whites until foamy and add them to the mixture. Put the mixture in a casserole dish buttered and sprinkled with bread crumbs. Dot with butter and bake in the oven for 30-35 minutes (until the surface is lightly brown and the casserole pulls away from the sides of the dish). Invert the casserole dish to remove the dessert. Slice and serve it hot or cold with fruit or berry sauces.

Cottage cheese with milk

300 g (10.5 oz) dry cottage cheese,
500 g (17.5 oz) milk,
sugar,
cinnamon

Distribute the cottage cheese among dessert plates, add milk, sugar and cinnamon, and serve for breakfast or as a dessert.

Cottage cheese patties

300 g (10.5 oz) dry cottage cheese,
2 eggs,
50 g (1.75 oz) flour,
10 g manna-croup,
20 g (0.7 oz) sugar,
salt, grated zest of 1 lemon,
fat

Mix together cottage cheese, eggs, sugar, salt, lemon zest, manna-croup and 30 g (1.05 oz) of the flour. Mix well. Spread the mixture on a floured board and roll out into a circle that is 3-4 centimeters in diameter. Cut pieces 2 cm (0.8 inches) thick. Dredge in flour and shape them with your hands so that they are round and flat. Put the patties in a greased casserole dish and bake in a medium oven until the cottage cheese is heated through and the patties are nicely brown.

Cottage cheese sticks

200 g (7 oz) dry cottage cheese,
1 egg,
2 tablespoons flour, salt,
potato starch,
vegetable oil

Process or grind the cottage cheese. Mix it with egg, flour and salt. Brush your fingers with potato starch and shape the cottage cheese mixture into "sticks" (about the thickness of an adult finger and approximately 5 cm (2 inches) long). Deep fry them until they are light brown. Serve with chicken dishes.

Summer solstice (*Jāņu*) cheese (mild cheese with caraway)

First version:
1 kg (2 lb, 3 oz) whole milk dry cottage cheese,
50 g (1.75 oz) milk,
50-75 g (1.75-2.625 oz) sour cream,
2 eggs,
50-75 g (1.75-2.625 oz) butter,
salt,
caraway seeds

Second version:
1 kg (2 lb, 3 oz) skim milk dry cottage cheese,
5 l milk,
100 g (3.5 oz) sour cream,
2 eggs,
100 g (3.5 oz) butter,
salt, caraway seeds

Heat the milk, stirring occasionally, to medium high temperature of 90-95°C (194-203°F). Process or grind the cottage cheese and add it to the milk. Heat at medium-low temperature of 85-90°C (185-194°F) for 10-15 minutes, until the whey separates from the cottage cheese. Remove the pot from the heat and allow the cottage cheese to sit. Pour off any liquid. Place cottage cheese in dampened cheesecloth. Gather the corners together, and roll the cheese back and forth to allow as much liquid as possible to separate out. Put the cottage cheese in a bowl. Mix the sour cream with the eggs, salt and caraway seeds and add it gradually to the cottage cheese. Mix well. Melt the butter in a pot. Put the cottage cheese over a low flame, stirring all the time, until smooth and shiny, and has a medium temperature of 75-80°C (167-176°F). (The lower the temperature and shorter the heating time, the softer and more crumbly the cheese will be. At a higher temperature and a longer heating time, it will become harder.) Place the cheese in a dampened cheesecloth. Tie the corners of the cloth together and put the cheese under a weight in the refrigerator. When the cheese has cooled remove it from the cloth and slice it. Summer solstice cheese is served with butter or honey or as a snack with beer. If you wish to store the cheese for a longer period of time, rub it with salt, wrap in cellophane and store in a cool, dry place. If you like, spread butter on the cheese and bake it in a hot oven until it is nicely browned.

Little cheeses

1 kg (2 lb, 3 oz) dry cottage cheese,
100 g (3.5 oz) sour cream,
salt,
caraway seeds

Process or grind the cottage cheese and add all of the other ingredients to it. Knead it thoroughly. Divide the mixture into small pieces, each with 75-100 g (3.5 oz) of mixture, and shape them into cones. Place cheese on a wooden board and cover with a clean cloth. Set aside in a warm place (18-20°C or 64-68°F) for a couple of days. When the cheese is covered with a transparent white layer, remove the cloth and put the cheese in a cool room to dry it. If you want to keep the cheese for a longer period of time, dry it more thoroughly and grate it before serving. These cheeses are eaten on sandwiches or as a snack with beer.

Cottage cheese with fruit

> 200 g (7 oz) dry cottage cheese,
> 100 g (3.5 oz) fruit or berries (strawberries,
>   raspberries, apricots, plums, etc., some of
>   the fruit candied),
> 50 g (1.75 oz) sweet cream,
> 50 g (1.75 oz) sugar,
> grated zest of 1 lemon

Grate the cottage cheese or press it through a sieve. Add 35 g of the sugar and the lemon zest and stir until the sugar has dissolved. Whip the cream. Add whipped cream and candied fruit to the mixture. Decorate with extra whipped cream and fresh fruit or berries.

Boiled cheese

> 1 kg (2 lb, 3 oz) dry cottage cheese,
> 75 g (2.625 oz) butter,
> 100 g (3.5 oz) milk or sweet cream,
> 1 egg,
> salt,
> caraway seeds

Process or grind the cottage cheese and mix it together with all of the other ingredients except the butter. Melt the butter in a pot, put the mixture in it and heat, stirring all the while, until the mixture is smooth and shiny. Place the cheese in a greased bowl and in the refrigerator to allow the cheese to harden.

Latgale cheese

> 5 l (5 quarts + 1 cup) unpasteurized whole
>   milk,
> salt

Take 3 liters of naturally soured milk. Heat until the whey separates. Add the remaining milk and, stirring occasionally. Heat until the milk has curdled. Allow the cheese to sit for a while and then drain it in a sieve. While it is still warm, wrap it in cheese cloth, weight it down in the refrigerator and store for 5-6 hours. Slice the cheese and serve it with sandwiches. If you want to keep the cheese for a longer period of time, rub its surface with salt, weight it down and let it dry out.

PANCAKES

Latvian pancakes are similar to Swedish pancakes
or crêpes. They are light and golden in colour.

Thin pancakes stuffed with meat

120 g (4.2 oz) flour,
240 g (8.4 oz) milk,
1 egg,
sugar, salt,
butter for cooking

For the stuffing:
100-150 g (3.5-5.25 oz) ground cooked beef,
20 g (0.7 oz) smoked bacon,
30 g (1.05 oz) onion,
salt,
beef stock

Prepare the thin pancakes as described
above. For the stuffing, chop the bacon and
onion, sauté. Add the ground beef and salt,
adding a little beef stock. Stir and heat through.
Stuff the pancakes, cook them as directed and
serve them with bouillon or vegetable soup.
These pancakes are delicious with loganberry
preserves and tea.

Thin pancakes (1-2 servings)

100 g (3.5 oz) flour,
200-240 g (7-8.4 oz) milk,
2 eggs,
10 g (0.35 oz) butter,
salt, sugar,
melted butter for cooking

Beat together the eggs, sugar and salt, add
3/4 of the milk, sift the flour into the liquid and
stir well. Add the rest of the milk. Melt the butter and add it to the dough. Stir until you get a
liquid dough and set aside for 25-30 minutes.
Heat a cast iron pan (16-18 cm (6.4-7.2 inches)
in diameter) and spread melted butter in it. Pour
the dough in the pan and swirl it to create a very
thin (2 mm) pancake. When the bottom is done,
flip the pancake and cook the other side. Fold
the pancakes in half or in quarters and serve with
jam, tea or coffee.

Pancakes filled with sweetened cottage cheese

120 g (4.2 oz) sifted flour,
240 g (8.4 oz) milk,
1 egg, sugar, salt,
fat for cooking

For the filling:
100 g (3.5 oz) skim milk dry cottage cheese,
1 egg,
10 g (0.35 oz) flour,
30 g (1.05 oz) sugar,
vanilla sugar or grated zest of 1 lemon,
20 g (0.7 oz) raisins

Alternative filling:
150 g (5.25 oz) skim milk dry cottage cheese,
20 g (0.7 oz) sour cream,
1 egg,
10 g (0.35 oz) flour,
10 g (0.35 oz) sugar,
caraway seeds, salt

Beat the egg with salt and sugar and add 3/4 of the milk. Gradually add the liquid to the sifted flour in a bowl, and stir until the dough is uniform. Add the additional milk and set aside for 20-30 minutes. Cook thin pancakes on one side and then put them on a wooden board or a shallow plate with the cooked side up. Place filling on one side of the pancake, fold over and cook until golden brown and the cottage cheese is warmed through.

For the filling: Process or grind the cottage cheese and mix it with all of the other ingredients. Serve the pancakes with sugar and cinnamon, melted butter or sour cream.

Thin pancakes stuffed with mushrooms

100 g (3.5 oz) flour, 250 g (8.75 oz) milk,
3 eggs, salt, butter

For the stuffing:
200 g (7 oz) mushrooms (preferably fresh picked),
30 g (1.05 oz) onion,
30 g (1.05 oz) butter,
salt, pepper,
50 g (1.75 oz) sweet cream,
chopped parsley

Prepare the thin pancakes as directed above. For the stuffing: Chop the onions and sauté in butter. Clean and chop the mushrooms and blanch in boiling water. Add them to the pan and sauté until all of the liquid has evaporated. Sprinkle with salt and pepper, add the cream and heat through. Sprinkle with chopped parsley. Stuff the pancakes, drizzle with melted butter and heat them in the oven.

Carrot pancakes

150 g (5.25 oz) flour,
150 g (5.25 oz) milk,
2 eggs,
200 g (7 oz) carrot,
10 g sugar,
salt, butter

Prepare the pancake dough as directed above. Add finely grated carrots and whipped egg whites and stir. Cook on a greased pan.

Potato pancakes

First version:
500 g (17.5 oz) potato,
1 egg,
40 g (1.4 oz) flour,
salt,
butter

Peel and rinse the potatoes and grate them finely. Add the egg, salt and flour and mix together. Cook on a greased pan until brown on both sides. Potato pancakes are usually dense, with the taste of raw potato. If you want the pancakes to be lighter in texture, then grate only 400 g (14 oz) of the potato and boil another 50 g (1.75 oz), pressing potato through a sieve before adding it to the mixture.

Second version:
500 g (17.5 oz) potato,
50 g (1.75 oz) sour cream,
baking soda,
10 g (0.35 oz) sugar,
salt,
1 egg,
20 g (0.7 oz) flour,
butter

Grind the potatoes and press them to extract as much liquid as possible. Mix the sour cream with the baking soda, and add with salt, sugar, egg and flour to the mixture. Cook on a greased pan. Work as quickly as possible. (Grated potatoes darken when exposed to the air.) Serve the pancakes hot from the pan with sour cream, bacon or lingonberry jam.

Thick egg pancakes

200 g (7 oz) flour,
200 g (7 oz) milk,
3 eggs,
100 g (3.5 oz) sugar,
salt,
grated zest of 1 lemon,
butter

Separate the eggs. Beat together the yolks with the sugar and lemon zest. Add the milk and a touch of salt. Gradually add the liquid to sifted flour. Stir until you get a uniform dough, and set aside for 25-30 minutes. Whip the egg whites and fold them into the dough. Spoon the pancakes onto a greased cast iron pan and cook on both sides until they are light brown. Serve with jam, tea or coffee.

Apple pancakes

150 g (5.25 oz) flour,
150 g (5.25 oz) sweet cream,
2 eggs,
30 g (1.05 oz) sugar,
salt,
200 g (7 oz) medium-tart apples,
butter

Separate the eggs. Beat together the egg yolks with sugar and salt. Add the cream, and blend in flour to get a uniform dough. Set aside for 25-30 minutes. Grate the apples or slice them thinly. Whip egg whites and add them to the dough along with the apples. Cook on a greased pan. Serve with sugar, cinnamon, honey and tea.

Pumpkin pancakes

150 g (5.25 oz) flour,
150 g (5.25 oz) milk,
20 g (0.7 oz) sugar,
salt,
grated zest of 1/2 lemon,
150 g (5.25 oz) pumpkin,
butter

To prepare the pumpkin: Grate the pumpkin into tiny slices, sprinkle with sugar and add lemon juice. Alternatively, grate the pumpkin more coarsely or cut it up into small pieces. Put it in a pot with water or milk. Add butter and steam until the pumpkin is soft. Press the pumpkin through a sieve and add the mixture to the dough.

Separate the eggs. Beat together the egg yolks with the sugar, salt and lemon zest. Add milk. Gradually pour the liquid into sifted flour, stirring to get a uniform dough. Set aside for 25-30 minutes. Whip the egg whites. Add egg whites and the pumpkin to the dough. Cook on a greased pan.

Cream pancakes

150 g (5.25 oz) flour,
150 g (5.25 oz) sour cream,
100 g (3.5 oz) dry cottage cheese,
3 eggs,
salt,
10 g (0.35 oz) sugar,
1/4 teaspoon baking soda,
fat

Mix together all of the ingredients and spoon the dough onto a greased cast iron pan, cooking on both sides until the pancakes are golden. Serve with loganberry jam or sour cream.

EGG DISHES

Eggs in cream (one serving)

1 egg,
40 g (1.4 oz) sour cream,
salt, sugar,
horseradish or mustard,
chopped parsley

Mix together all of the ingredients except the egg and the parsley. Boil the egg. Peel and cut egg in half. Put the sour cream mixture in a dish and lay the halves of the egg on top of it. Sprinkle with the chopped parsley.

Farmer's breakfast

2 eggs,
30 g (1.05 oz) milk,
salt,
75 g (2.625 oz) smoked pork or 50 g (1.75 oz) smoked bacon,
25 g (0.875 oz) sausage,
15 g (0.525 oz) onion,
100-120 g (3.5-4.2 oz) boiled potato

Cut the smoked meat or bacon and the sausage into bite-sized pieces and chop the onion. Sauté the onion and meats in butter. Meanwhile, slice the boiled potatoes and add them to the pan. When they are browned on both sides, beat together the eggs and milk. Pour it into the casserole dish, and bake in the oven until the eggs are firm. Serve with a salad of lettuce, cucumber or tomato.

Tomatoes stuffed with scrambled eggs

2 medium tomatoes,
2 eggs,
1 tablespoon chopped dill,
1 tablespoon butter,
salt

Cut the tops of the tomatoes and set aside. Scoop out their insides. Put the tomatoes on a board, cut side down, so that their juice drains out. Meanwhile beat eggs with salt and chopped dill. Melt half of the butter in a pan and pour in the eggs. Stir and heat until the scrambled eggs are firm. Remove from the heat. Sprinkle salt into the tomatoes and stuff them with the scrambled eggs. Put the tops of the tomatoes back on. Put the remaining butter in a casserole dish. Add the tomatoes and heat them in the oven for 5-10 minutes.

Eggs in herring sauce

*2 hard-boiled eggs. For the sauce: 75 g
(2.625 oz) salted herring,
8 g (0.3 oz) vegetable oil,
5 g (0.175 oz) vinegar,
2 g mustard,
10 g (0.35 oz) onion,
15 g (0.525 oz) sour cream,
green onion*

For the herring sauce: Soak the salted herring in cold water for 4-6 hours. Skin and clean the fish. Cut the filets into small pieces. Mix all ingredients together.

Peel the eggs and slice them in half lengthwise. Place eggs in a bowl. Pour the herring sauce over them and sprinkle chopped green onion on top.

Omelet with ham

*2 eggs,
40 g (1.4 oz) milk,
15 g (0.525 oz) butter, salt*

*For the filling:
150 g (5.25 oz) ham,
2 tablespoons sweet cream or 30 g (1.05 oz)
butter*

Beat the eggs, adding salt and milk. Melt the butter in a pan, pour in the eggs and cook until the omelet is ready. Take it off the flame and allow it to cool.

Filling: Grind the ham. Whip butter thoroughly before adding it to the ham. Otherwise, add the cream. Spread this mixture over the omelet and roll it up. Wrap in baking paper and keep in the refrigerator for a few hours. Remove the roll from the baking paper. Slice and serve as a cold snack or for sandwiches. Add chopped parsley or dill to the eggs before beating them. For the filling try cream cheese mixed with diced smoked cod or mackerel.

Omelet with fruit

*2 eggs,
15 g (0.525 oz) sweet cream,
5 g (0.175 oz) sugar,
salt,
lemon zest,
75 g (2.625 oz) fruit (strawberry, raspberry,
cherry) or apple jam,
15 g (0.525 oz) butter*

Separate the eggs and grate the lemon zest. Whip the egg yolks together with the sugar and the lemon zest. Add the sweet cream and a touch of salt, and mix well. Whip the egg whites in a separate bowl. Fold them into the mixture. Melt butter in a casserole dish, pour in the eggs, and bake in the oven at a low temperature. Allow to bake until a golden brown. Remove the omelet from the oven, put sweet filling in its center, fold it over and sprinkle with powdered sugar. Serve with tea or coffee.

Eggs with smoked pork

2 eggs,
75 g (2.625 oz) smoked pork,
2 slices tomato,
2 rings of an onion,
salt, pepper, mustard,
butter

Cut the pork into two thin slices, brush it with mustard and fry in butter on one side. Remove the meat from the pan. Cook onion and tomato. Return meat to the pan, uncooked side down. Put one of the onion rings and one of the slices of tomato on each piece of meat. Beat together eggs with salt and pepper. Pour them over the tomato slices. Cover the pan and simmer over a low flame until ready. Serve for dinner with boiled potatoes and buttermilk.

Stuffed eggs (1 serving)

1 egg,
10 g (0.35 oz) butter or sour cream,
mustard, salt, lemon juice or vinegar, sugar

For decoration:
2 small sprats,
radishes, tomatoes, chopped herbs

Boil the egg. Peel and carefully cut it lengthwise. Remove the yolk. Put the yolk through a sieve. In a mixing bowl, add egg yolk, butter, salt, mustard, vinegar and sugar and beat well. Fill the egg whites with the mixture. Decorate with sprats and slices of radish. Arrange on lettuce leaves to serve.

DESSERTS

Strawberries with milk

400 g (14 oz) strawberries,
60 g (2.1 oz) powdered sugar,
300 g (10.5 oz) milk

Clean the strawberries and rinse them in cold water. Drain. Arrange them in dessert dishes. Serve the powdered sugar and milk on the side. Substitute raspberries. For blueberries, sprinkle with sugar first. Serve with milk.

Apple "crowns"

200 g (7 oz) apple,
6 g sugar,
50 g (1.75 oz) butter,
powdered sugar

For the dough:
50 g (1.75 oz) flour,
1 egg,
50 g (1.75 oz) milk,
10 g (0.35 oz) sugar,
20 g (0.7 oz) sweet cream

To make the dough: Separate the egg. Beat the yolk together with sugar, cream and some of the milk. Sift the flour and add it to the liquid, stirring to form a uniform dough. Add the remaining milk, mix well and allow the dough to stand for 30 minutes. Peel and core the apples, slice them into rounds that are 1/2-1 cm (0.2-0.4 inches) thick. Sprinkle with sugar. Whip the egg white and fold into the dough. Dip the apple slices into the dough and brown them in butter in a cast iron pan. Arrange them in a dish and sprinkle with powdered sugar. Serve hot with milk.

Pumpkin in quince juice with whipped cream

300 g (10.5 oz) pumpkin,
3 tablespoons quince juice,
1 tablespoon honey,
2 tablespoons sugar,
1/2 glass oats (not instant),
1 teaspoon butter,
1 teaspoon sugar,
150 g (5.25 oz) sweet cream,
3 teaspoons sugar

Mix the oats with the first portion of sugar. Melt butter in a pan and toast the sugared oats until they are golden. Allow to cool. Peel and slice the pumpkin. Mix it with the honey (warm honey first if it does not mix easily). Add sugar and the juice. Set aside for 30 minutes. Serve the pumpkin with sweetened whipped cream (adding second portion of sugar for whipping cream). Sprinkle with toasted oats.

Whipped cream with baked apples

400 g (14 oz) medium-tart apples,
200 g (7 oz) sweet cream,
80 g (2.8 oz) sugar

Wash and core the apples. Sprinkle sugar inside apples and bake in the oven. Don't allow apples to fall apart. Baked apples can be served hot or cold — with milk if hot and with the whipped cream or vanilla sauce, if they are cold. You may also use vanilla sauce.

Cottage cheese dumplings

200 g (7 oz) dry cottage cheese,
1 teaspoon sour cream,
1/2 egg, 1 teaspoon sugar,
grated zest of 1 lemon

For the dough:
1 glass flour, 1/2 egg,
1/4 glass water, 1/2 teaspoon vegetable oil

For the stuffing: Process or grind the dry cottage cheese, add the grated lemon zest, egg, sour cream and sugar, and mix well.

Mix together all of the dough ingredients to form a uniform dough. Set aside for one hour in the refrigerator. On a flat surface, roll out the dough into a thin layer. Starting at the corners, put a teaspoonful or so of filling at one edge of the dough, fold over and press out a round shape with two layers of dough and the filling in between. Boil the dumplings in lightly salted water. When they rise to the top, remove them from the pot with a slotted spoon. Serve warm with melted butter or allow to cool and serve with fruit soup.

Pumpkin in cranberry juice

300 g (10.5 oz) pumpkin,
50 g (1.75 oz) cranberries,
1-2 tablespoons sugar,
1/2 tablespoon honey

Blanch the cranberries in boiling water. Let them cool. Grind or process cranberries. Add honey and sugar and stir until the sugar has dissolved. Peel and slice pumpkin. Add the cranberry mixture to it and mix well. Let the pumpkin set for an hour the flavors to blend. Serve with whipped cream. Carrots can be prepared in the same way.

Bread soup

300 g (10.5 oz) dark rye bread,
4 glasses water,
80 g (2.8 oz) sugar,
50 g (1.75 oz) dried fruit (raisins, apples,
  prunes),
40 g (1.4 oz) cranberries,
cinnamon,
70 g (2.45 oz) sweet cream,
sugar

Slice the rye bread and toast in the oven. Put the toasted bread into a bowl, pour 4 glasses of boiling water over it to cover. Cover the bowl and set aside for 30 minutes. Put the bread and the liquid through a sieve. Pour the resulting mixture into a pot. Add sugar, dried fruit and cinnamon, and cook until the fruit is soft. Squeeze the cranberries to get their juice. Serve the soup cold. Put a few ice cubes in each bowl, pour the soup over and top with whipped cream.

99

Biguzis

> 200 g (7 oz) dark rye bread,
> 140 g (4.9 oz) water,
> 60 g (2.1 oz) cranberry juice,
> 1 tablespoon sugar,
> 1 tablespoon honey,
> 60 g (2.1 oz) sweet cream,
> 1 teaspoon sugar

Boil the water with sugar. Add the honey and cranberry juice, and allow to cool. Remove the crust from the bread. Cube the bread, place into dessert dishes. Pour the liquid over it and set aside for 30 minutes for the flavors to blend. Serve with whipped cream.

Fruit soup

> 200 g (7 oz) apple,
> 10 g (0.35 oz) prunes,
> 600 g (21 oz) water,
> 80 g (2.8 oz) sugar,
> 40 g (1.4 oz) cranberries,
> 8 g (0.3 oz) potato starch

Peel the apples and cut them into neat slices. Remove the core. Do not discard. Rinse cranberries and press out all of their juice. Boil the apple peels, apple cores and crushed cranberries in little water. Strain the water, adding soaked prunes and sugar, and bring to a boil. Dissolve potato starch in water and add to the liquid. Return to a boil, stirring constantly. Add the apples slices. Remove the pot from the flame. Add the juice, cover the pot and allow to cool. Fruit soup can be served with cottage cheese dumplings.

Carrot dessert

> 200 g (7 oz) carrot,
> 400 g (14 oz) water,
> 60-80 g sugar,
> 30 g (1.05 oz) potato starch,
> berry or lemon juice

Boil the water. Meanwhile, finely grate the carrots. Put them in the water and cook until they are tender. Add sugar, along with cranberry, currant or lemon juice. Adde potato starch (which dissolved in some cold water). Bring to a boil. Pour into serving dishes, and sprinkle with sugar. Allow to cool and serve with milk. This dessert should have a sweet, tart taste (the more lemon juice you add, the more sugar you will need).

Pumpkin dessert

> 180 g pumpkin,
> 25 g (0.875 oz) butter,
> 250 g (8.75 oz) milk,
> 50 g (1.75 oz) sugar,
> 20 g (0.7 oz) potato starch,
> vanillin

Peel the pumpkin and remove its seeds. Grate pumpkin and sauté in the butter over a low flame until it is tender. Put the pumpkin through a sieve, add the milk, sugar and vanillin. Return to the stove and return to boiling. Dissolve the potato starch in some water or milk. Add it to the pot and bring to the boil again. Pour into dessert dishes. Allow to cool and serve with cranberry sauce.

Milk dessert

> *400 g (14 oz) milk,*
> *60 g (2.1 oz) sugar,*
> *20 g (0.7 oz) hazelnuts or almonds,*
> *30 g (1.05 oz) potato starch,*
> *vanillin*

Toast the nuts in the oven. Chop or grind nuts in processor. Bring milk to a boil. Add sugar, ground nuts, vanillin and potato starch (first dissolving in some milk). Cook the dessert over a low flame, stirring with a wooden spoon. Pour the dessert into dessert plates, sprinkle with extra chopped nuts, and allow it to cool. Serve with cranberry sauce. For a lighter dessert, replace half of the potato starch with flour. Add a split and seeded vanilla pod to the milk while it is cooking, removing it when the dish is done.

Sorrel desert

> *200 g (7 oz) sorrel,*
> *1 l (1 quart + 4 tablespoons) water,*
> *160 g (5.6 oz) sugar,*
> *2 tablespoons potato starch,*
> *salt*

Cut up the sorrel and sauté it in a bit of water. Add salt, stir and cook until the sorrel is tender. Put it through a sieve. Add the rest of the water and the sugar and cook for 3 minutes. Dissolve the potato starch in some water and add it to the liquid. Pour the dessert into bowls, allow it to cool and serve with milk.

Apple jelly

> *400 g (14 oz) apple juice,*
> *12 g gelatin,*
> *50 g (1.75 oz) sweet cream,*
> *10 g (0.35 oz) sugar,*
> *vanillin*

Pour the gelatin into half of the apple juice. Heat the other half of the juice to boiling. Add the juice with the gelatin and stir to dissolve. Allow to cool a bit. Pour into ramekins and allowing the jelly to set. Serve with whipped cream. You may prepare jelly from other juices, as well. Apple jelly is traditionally served with roast pork dishes.

Cranberry dessert (*ķīselis*)

> *100 g (3.5 oz) cranberries,*
> *400 g (14 oz) water,*
> *60 g (2.1 oz) sugar,*
> *30 g (1.05 oz) potato starch*

Rinse the berries. Crush them and press out all of their juice. Put the berry skins in boiling water and boil for 5 minutes. Strain. Add the sugar and the potato starch to the liquid. Add starch (dissolved in water). Bring to a boil. Add the juice you have collected from the cranberries and stir well. Pour the mixture into dessert dishes, sprinkle with sugar and let it cool thoroughly. Make this dessert with currents.

(If the dessert is not very firm, serve it with whipped cream. If it is quite firm, you can also serve it with ice cream.)

Blueberry soup with dumplings

240 g (8.4 oz) blueberries,
80 g (2.8 oz) sugar,
8 g (0.3 oz) potato starch,
grated zest of 1 lemon,
pinch lemon juice,
600 g (21 oz) wate

Dumplings:
60 g (2.1 oz) flour,
30 g (1.05 oz) milk,
1 egg, salt, sugar

Boil a little water. Add the sugar, lemon zest and rinsed blueberries and cook until the berries are somewhat disintegrated. Add the lemon juice and potato starch (dissolved in water first), bring to a boil again until thickened and allow to cool.

Dumplings: Mix the egg together with the milk (use cream if you like), and add it to the flour, along with the salt and sugar. Mix thoroughly. Form dumplings with a spoon and boil in salted water until ready. Drain them and add to the soup before serving.

Whipped apples

First version:
100 g (3.5 oz) apples,
160 g (5.6 oz) water,
50 g (1.75 oz) sugar,
300 g (10.5 oz) manna-croup

Peel, core and slice apples. Put them in a pot, cover with water and cook until the apples are all but falling apart. Put them through a sieve. Add sugar and manna-croup to the apple mixture and return to the stove to continue cooking. Stir all the while until the manna-croup is thickened. Cool the mixture a little. Beat warm apples thoroughly to form foamy peaks. Serve with milk.

Second version:
200 g (7 oz) apple,
50 g (1.75 oz) sugar,
1 egg white

Bake the apples in the oven, put them through a sieve, add the sugar and stir well. Allow the mixture to cool entirely. Add the egg white and whip to firm, foamy peaks. Put the whipped dessert into dessert dishes and serve with vanilla sauce or whipped cream.

Serve this dessert in a long dessert glasses by putting a scoop of ice cream in the glass first, then a layer of the apple dessert, then some whipped cream and, finally, some vanilla sauce.

Sour cream jelly

200 g (7 oz) sour cream,
50 g (1.75 oz) sugar,
6 g (0.2 oz) gelatin,
vanillin or grated zest of 1 lemon

Add all of the ingredients except the gelatin to the sour cream and stir well. Put the gelatin into some warm water and allow it to dissolve. Add it to the sour cream mixture. Pour the mixture into ramekins and allow it to set. Serve with cranberry sauce.

Whipped cranberry dessert (*debesmanna*)

> *75 g (2.625 oz) cranberries,*
> *200 g (7 oz) water,*
> *50 g (1.75 oz) sugar,*
> *30 g (1.05 oz) manna-croup*

Rinse cranberries. Crush them and press out all of their juice. Pour water over the cranberry solids, boil for 5 minutes and strain. Add the sugar to the cooking liquid. Gradually add the manna-croup, stirring constantly. Heat until the manna-croup thickens and then add the cranberry juice. Put the mixture into a bowl and cool as quickly as possible. Using a mixer, whip until mixture is light and airy. It will double or triple in volume while you do this, so use a large mixing bowl. Serve in deep, dessert dishes with cold milk. Currants, gooseberries and other berries can be used in the same way, but only cranberry dessert is called *debesmanna*.

Whipped rhubarb

> *250 g (8.75 oz) rhubarb,*
> *60 g (2.1 oz) sugar,*
> *2 egg whites,*
> *grated zest of 1 lemon*

Wash, peel and chop the rhubarb. Sauté together with the sugar until very tender. Strain through a sieve. Allow the mixture to cool. Add the egg white and the lemon zest and beat in a mixer to form stiff, foamy peaks. Serve with vanilla sauce or whipped cream.

Chocolate cream

> First version:
> *100 g (3.5 oz) sweet cream,*
> *12 g (0.42 oz) cocoa,*
> *30 g (1.05 oz) sugar,*
> *40 g (1.4 oz) milk,*
> *1 egg yolk,*
> *4 g (0.15 oz) gelatin*

Beat egg yolk together with sugar and add cocoa. Heat milk and gradually add it to the egg mixture, stirring continuously. Put the gelatin in water and allow it to stand. Add it to the hot mixture. Stir to dissolve, and allow the mixture to cool. Whip the cream, adding the egg mixture. Stir. Pour into a bowl and allow the dessert to set. Serve with extra whipped cream.

> Second version:
> *12 g (0.42 oz) cocoa,*
> *20 g (0.7 oz) sugar,*
> *40 g (1.4 oz) milk,*
> *1/2 egg yolk,*
> *200 g (7 oz) ice cream,*
> *6 g (0.21 oz) gelatin*

Beat the egg yolk together with sugar and add cocoa. Heat milk and gradually add it to the egg mixture, stirring until it thickens. Pour the gelatin in a little water and allow it to stand. Add it to the egg mixture and stir to dissolve. Allow the mixture to cool. Add ice cream and whip the mixture thoroughly. Pour it into dessert dishes. Allow it to set. Sprinkle with grated chocolate before serving.

Pumpkin cream

First version:
200 g (7 oz) pumpkin,
80 g (2.8 oz) sugar,
lemon juice (1/2 lemon),
zest of 1/2 lemon,
* 10 g (0.35 oz) cognac,*
100 g (3.5 oz) sweet cream,
12 g (0.42 oz) gelatin

Peel and dice the pumpkin. Sauté it in a bit of water until it is tender and then put it through a sieve. Add sugar, grated lemon zest, lemon juice and the cognac. Add the gelatin (having first allowed it to sit in water). Heat the mixture until the gelatin dissolves. Allow the mixture to cool. Whip the cream and mix the pumpkin mixture into it. Pour the mixture into dessert dishes and allow it to set. Serve with vanilla sauce, if you wish.

Second version:
200 g (7 oz) pumpkin,
140 g (4.9 oz) medium-tart apple,
60 g (2.1 oz) sugar,
100 g (3.5 oz) sweet cream,
cinnamon,
16 g (0.56 oz) gelatin

Peel and core the pumpkin and apples. Grate them finely. Soak them in a bit of water and sauté until they are tender (and all of the water has evaporated). Put the pumpkin and apples through a sieve. Add sugar, cinnamon and dissolved gelatin. When the mixture has cooled, whip the cream and stir it in.

Vanilla or egg cream

1 egg yolk,
30 g (1.05 oz) sugar,
100 g (3.5 oz) sweet cream,
40 g (1.4 oz) milk,
4 g (0.15 oz) gelatin,
vanillin

Beat the egg yolk together with the sugar and vanillin. Boil the milk and add it gradually to the egg mixture, stirring continuously. Put the dish in a bath of hot water and heat until thick (this should occur at a temperature of between 70 and 80°C, or 158 and 176°F). Pour gelatin into a little water and set aside. Add it to the hot mixture and stir until the gelatin is dissolved. Cool the mixture just until warm. Whip the sweet cream and add it to the mixture. Pour the mixture into a dish and allow it to cool completely. Serve with fruit or berry syrup.

Rhubarb cream

250 g (8.75 oz) rhubarb,
60 g (2.1 oz) sugar,
grated zest of 1 lemon,
120 g (4.2 oz) sweet cream,
4 g (0.15 oz) gelatin

Peel and cut the rhubarb. Sauté with sugar until very tender. Add the lemon zest and the dissolved gelatin. When the mixture is cool, whip the cream and fold it in. Allow the mixture to set. Serve in broad-rimmed wine glasses with sweet cream syrup.

Dried fruit cream

50 g (1.75 oz) dried fruit (pitted prunes),
200 g (7 oz) water,
40 g (1.4 oz) sugar,
100 g (3.5 oz) sweet cream,
20 g (0.7 oz) chopped hazelnuts,
2-3 g (0.07-0.1 oz) gelatin

Rinse the dried fruit and place in a pot. Add water and sugar, simmering slowly until the fruit becomes very soft. Put the fruit through a sieve and cool in refrigerator. Whip the cream, adding the dissolved gelatin to it while you are whipping. Then add the fruit. Toast the chopped nuts and add them to the mixture. Allow dessert to set. Serve in dessert dishes with a drop of sweet cream syrup.

Flour pudding

40 g (1.4 oz) flour,
200 g (7 oz) milk, 2 eggs,
30 g (1.05 oz) sugar, vanillin

Mix the flour with one-third of the milk. Put the rest of the milk in a pot along with vanillin and bring to a boil. Add it to the flour mixture, put the mixture back on the stove and heat quickly to boiling, stirring continuously. Reduce the heat and simmer for 5 minutes over a low flame. Whip the egg yolk with the sugar and add it to the flour mixture. Allow it to cool slightly to 70°C (158°F). Whip the egg whites to stiff peaks and carefully fold them into the pudding. Serve in deep dessert dishes with cranberry sauce.

Rye bread cream

160 g (5.6 oz) sweet cream,
40-50 g (1.4-1.75 oz) dark dry rye bread,
2 g (0.07 oz) gelatin,
60 g (2.1 oz) raspberry or strawberry jam

Whip the cream. Grate the rye bread into fine crumbs. Add rye bread and the dissolved gelatin to the cream and carefully fold in the jam. Serve with vanilla sauce or milk.

Floating islands

300 g (10.5 oz) milk,
2 eggs,
50 g (1.75 oz) sugar,
vanillin or 1-2 vanilla beans

Separate the eggs. Whip the egg whites with half of the sugar to firm peaks. Heat the milk. Using a large spoon, drop egg whites in portions into the milk, cooking and stirring 3-5 minutes. Remove the "islands" from the milk and arrange them in deep dessert dishes. Do not discard milk. Whip the egg yolks with the remaining sugar. Add vanillin to the milk in which the egg whites cooked. Heat, stirring, until the sauce becomes a bit thicker. Pour over the "islands" in the dessert plates. (You may also put the sauce in the plates first, and then add the egg whites.) Serve cold. If you use vanilla beans, split them, seed them and boil them with the milk.

Traditional Latvian ambrosia

First version:
*150 g (5.25 oz) dry,
dark rye bread,
100 g (3.5 oz) loganberry jam,
40 g (1.4 oz) sugar,
cinnamon,
120 g (4.2 oz) sweet cream,
vanillin*

Finely grate the rye bread and mix with the cinnamon and one-half of the sugar. Whip the cream, adding the sugar and vanillin gradually. Whip until you get stiff peaks. In a shallow dish, arrange the ingredients in layers: the rye bread, then the jam, then the whipped cream, then the rye bread again, etc. Make the rye bread the top layer and decorate with whipped cream. Serve with milk in a separate glass.

Second version:
*160-200 g (5.6-7 oz) dry,
dark rye bread,
40 g (1.4 oz) sugar,
30 g (1.05 oz) butter,
100 g (3.5 oz) loganberry jam,
120 g (4.2 oz) sweet cream,
vanillin*

Finely grate the rye bread. Mix with half of the sugar, and brown in melted butter, stirring frequently. Allow it to cool. Whip the cream with the remaining sugar and vanillin. Layer the ingredients as above. Serve with milk.

Sweet rye bread casserole

*200 g (7 oz) dry,
dark rye bread,
200 g (7 oz) apple,
50 g (1.75 oz) sugar,
cinnamon,
50 g (1.75 oz) butter,
100 g (3.5 oz) milk,
1/2 egg*

Finely grate the rye bread and mix it with the cinnamon and one-half of the sugar. Peel, core and slice the apple. Butter an ovenproof dish and layer the rye bread and apple slices, starting with the rye bread and topping each layer with sugar and dots of butter. Make the rye bread the last layer. Beat together the half egg and the milk and pour it over the bread and apples. Bake in a moderate oven for 30-40 minutes, covered for the 15-20 minutes of that time. Serve hot or cold with milk in a separate glass.

Whipped loganberry preserves

*300 g (10.5 oz) loganberry jam,
2 egg whites*

Add the egg whites to the jam and beat until stiff. Alternatively, whip the egg whites separately and carefully fold into the jam. Serve with milk. Use strawberry, plum and other jam for this dessert.

Cream pudding

100 g (3.5 oz) sour cream,
2 tablespoons flour,
2 eggs,
50 g (1.75 oz) sugar,
1 teaspoon butter,
grated zest of 1 lemon

Mix the flour and sugar into sour cream. Bring mixture to a boil, stirring constantly. Allow to cool. Separate the eggs. Add the egg yolks and lemon zest to the mixture. Whip the egg whites to stiff peaks and fold them in. Butter on ovenproof dish, pour the mixture into it and bake in a medium oven for 25-30 minutes. Serve hot or cold with berry or chocolate sauce.

BREADS, PASTRY
AND
CAKES

Yeast breads

There are two ways to make bread dough: with a starter and without a starter. One specific type of yeast-based dough is layered dough. Butter is put between layers of the dough so that after baking, the result is layered, with the specific taste and aroma of butter.

> *100 g (3.5 oz) yeast,*
> *150 g (5.25 oz) water,*
> *25 g (0.875 oz) sifted flour*

Preparing dough without a starter: Mix yeast with warm water and a bit of sifted flour and put it in a warm place to rise for 15-20 minutes. Heat water or milk to low temperature 35°C (95°F). Dissolve salt and sugar in it and add beaten eggs, yeast and sifted flour. Stir until you have a uniform dough. Beat some butter until it is soft and add it to the dough. Knead until the dough no longer sticks to your hands or the sides of the bowl. Sprinkle flour all across the dough, cover the bowl with a clean cloth, and put in a warm place to rise for 3 to 3 1/2 hours. After one hour, the dough should have nearly doubled in size. Punch it down with your fists before continuing the rising process. The rising process works best if the temperature of the dough is kept at between 25 and 30°C (77 and 86°F). The dough is ready when it has increased in volume by 2 to 2.5 times. (Press your thumb into the dough. The dough should return to its original shape slowly.)

Preparing dough with a starter: Heat water or milk at a low temperature 30-35°C (86-95°F). Add one-half of the sifted flour and the dissolved yeast, and stir until you get a thin dough. This is the starter. Cover it with a layer of flour that is 1/2-1 cm (0.2-0.4 inches) thick. Cover the bowl with a clean cloth, and allow to rise in a warm place for 1 to 1 1/2 hours. The starter is ready when it has doubled in size, when you can see cracks or air bubbles on the surface, and when it collapses to touch. Add the remaining flour to the starter, along with dissolved salt, butter (or vegetable oil) that you have whipped together with sugar and eggs (or just egg yolks). Add any spices that you need. Knead the dough until it is uniform and no longer sticks to your hands and the bowl. Even out the dough and sprinkle it with flour. Cover the bowl with a clean cloth and let the dough rise in a warm place for 1-2 hours. Punch the dough down once or twice during this process.

Preparing layered yeast dough: Prepare this dough with or without a starter. When the dough has risen, cool it to 18-20°C (64-68°F) and roll it out into a long piece that is 1 1/2 cm (0.6 inches) thick. Brush melted butter on two-thirds of the dough and then into thirds. Bring the part of the dough that is not covered with butter over the part that is, and then fold the remaining part of buttered dough over. This means that you have a block of dough with three layers of dough and two with butter. Press together the ends to avoid the butter dripping out. (Turn the dough by 90°.) Roll until it is 1 cm (0.4 inches) thick, and then fold it in four — bring the ends of the dough into the middle, and then fold the two sides over one another. If you have used a lot of butter, roll the dough out and fold it in three one more time. After the dough has been rolled and folded, put it in a cool place (6-8°C, or 42-46°F) and keep it there for 10-15 minutes. Use the dough to create various pastries (when putting them on the pan, leave space between the pieces of dough so that they do not stick together after rising and baking). When you have prepared the pastries and put them on the pan, cover them with a clean cloth and let them rise again (45-60 minutes for larger pastries, 15-20 minutes for smaller ones). Brush the pastries with a beaten egg or egg yolk. Bake larger pastries at 230-250°C (446-482°F) for 30-45 minutes, smaller ones at 250-280°C (482-536°F) for 10-15 minutes. Pastries are done when they are light brown and when a toothpick inserted in the center of the pastry comes out clean. If you want the crust to be softer, brush it with melted butter.

Barley rolls

0.8-1 kg (1.8-2.2 lb) coarse barley meal,
400 g (14 oz) milk,
50 g (1.75 oz) yeast,
25 g (0.875 oz) sugar,
100 g (3.5 oz) fat,
10 g salt,
250-300 g (8.75-10.5 oz) boiled potatoes

For the cottage cheese filling:
500 g (17.5 oz) dry cottage cheese,
150 g (5.25 oz) sour cream,
100 g (3.5 oz) sugar,
2 eggs

Prepare the dough with a starter. Towards the end of the kneading, put the boiled potatoes through a sieve and add them to the dough. When the dough is risen, form round rolls (8-10 cm (3.2-4 inches) in diameter), put them on a greased baking sheet and let them rise. Press an indentation in the middle of each roll, spoon some of the cottage cheese filing in it, brush with beaten egg, and bake.

For the filling: Mix all of the ingredients well.

Honey rolls

500 g (17.5 oz) coarse flour,
200 g (7 oz) milk,
25 g (0.875 oz) yeast,
50 g (1.75 oz) sugar, salt,
100 g (3.5 oz) butter,
150 g (5.25 oz) boiled potato

For the honey mixture:
100 g (3.5 oz) honey,
10 g (0.35 oz) butter,
100 g (3.5 oz) shelled hazelnuts,
2 egg yolks

Prepare the dough with a starter. Boil the potatoes and put them through a sieve. Add the potatoes and the butter to the starter, knead and let rise. Divide up the risen dough into pieces of 45-50 g (1.4-1.575 oz), roll them with your hands until they are round, put them on a greased baking sheet, and let them rise. Press an indentation into each roll, spoon in some of the honey mixture and bake.

For the honey mixture: Heat the butter and honey to boiling. Finely chop the nuts and add them to the mixture. Mix well and allow to cool. Then mix with the egg yolks.

Wheat rolls

0.8-1 kg coarse flour,
50 g (1.75 oz) yeast,
500 g (17.5 oz) milk,
25 g (0.875 oz) sugar,
50 g (1.75 oz) butter,
10 g salt

Prepare the dough without a starter. When the dough is risen, make small rolls (6-7 cm (2.4-2.8 inches) in diameter), put them on a greased baking sheet, let them rise, brush them with beaten egg and bake. These rolls are tasty with butter, honey and milk.

Caraway seed rolls

750 g (26.25 oz) flour,
200 g (7 oz) milk,
50 g (1.75 oz) yeast,
250 g (8.75 oz) butter,
100 g (3.5 oz) sugar,
2 eggs,
10 g (0.35 oz) salt,
50 g (1.75 oz) butter,
caraway seeds,
1 egg

Prepare the dough with a starter. When the dough rises, divide it into pieces of 45-50 g (1.4-1.575 oz). Use your hands to roll the dough into firm, round rolls. Place on a greased baking sheet and let dough rise for 10-15 minutes. Press an indentation into each roll. Let them rise a bit more, and brush with a beaten egg. Put a bit of butter into each indentation, sprinkle with caraway seeds, and bake in a medium oven.

Sklandu rolls

> 450-500 g (15.75-17.5 oz) coarse rye or
>   wheat flour,
> 200 g (7 oz) water,
> 50 g (1.75 oz) lard,
> 10 g (0.35 oz) sugar,
> salt,
> 1 egg

For the potato filling:
> 250 g (8.75 oz) potatoes,
> 25 g (0.875 oz) milk,
> 15 g (0.525 oz) butter,
> salt

For the carrot filling:
> 350-400 g (14 oz) carrot,
> 50 g (1.75 oz) sugar,
> salt,
> 25 g (0.875 oz) sour cream,
> 2 eggs,
> 15 g (0.525 oz) flour

Sift the flour, add the lard and mix with your fingers until crumbly. Heat the water to 20-25°C (68-77°F) and dissolve the sugar and salt in it. If you want, you can add 10-15 g (0.35-0.525 oz) yeast, too. Knead into a stiff dough that can easily be rolled. Roll out the dough until it is 2-3 mm thick and press out rounds (10-12 cm (4-4.8 inches) in diameter). Fold up the edges of each round to a height of 1-1 1/2 cm (0.4-0.6 inches). Put the rounds on a greased baking sheet. Spoon some potato mixture and then some carrot mixture into each of the rounds. Brush them with beaten egg, and bake in a medium oven for 10-15 minutes, until they are light brown and the dough is dry and crumbly.

For the potato mixture: Peel, boil and drain the potatoes. Put them through a sieve. Boil the milk with the butter, add it to the potatoes and mix well.

For the carrot mixture: Boil the carrots with their skins on. Peel them, put them through a sieve, add all of the other ingredients and mix well.

Sometimes *sklandu* rolls are baked just with the potato mixture or just with the carrot mixture. Sometimes people add grated fresh carrot, salt, sugar, eggs, sour cream and flour to the potatoes which have been pressed through the sieve before filling the rolls.

Water pretzels

> 550-600 g (19.25-21 oz) flour,
> 250 g (8.75 oz) water,
> 25 g (0.875 oz) yeast,
> 50-70 g (1.75-2.45 oz) butter,
> salt, caraway seeds

Prepare the dough with a starter. When the dough rises, roll it out, divide it into pieces of 45-50 g (1.4-1.575 oz), form pretzels and let them rise. Put the pretzels in boiling salt water, cooking them until they rise to the surface. Remove them from the water with a slotted spoon. Put them on a greased baking sheet. Sprinkle with caraway seeds and bake in a hot oven until they are light yellow.

Apple pastry

First version:
500 g (17.5 oz) flour,
250 g (8.75 oz) milk,
25 g (0.875 oz) yeast,
100 g (3.5 oz) butter,
100 g sugar,
2 eggs,
5 g (0.175 oz) salt,
800 g (28 oz) apples,
50 g (1.75 oz) sugar,
50 g (1.75 oz) butter,
cinnamon,
powdered sugar

Prepare the dough without a starter. When the dough has risen, roll it out to a thickness of 1 cm (0.4 inches) and put it on a greased baking sheet. Smooth the dough and let it rise. Peel and thinly slice the apples while the dough is rising. Arrange the apples in neat rows along the dough. Melt the butter and brush it over the apples. Mix sugar and cinnamon and sprinkle them over the apples. Bake in a medium oven until the crust is nicely browned and the apples are soft. Let the pastry cool. Sprinkle with powdered sugar, and slice.

The fresh apples can be replaced with dried apples (soaked in water before they are put on the dough). You may also pour a mixture of egg and cream over the apples before baking: Whip together 3 egg yolks with 100 g (3.5 oz) sugar, add 3/4 glass sour cream, the grated zest of one lemon, 1 tablespoon of melted butter, 3 beaten egg whites and 1 tablespoon of flour. Mix well.

Second version:
600 g (21 oz) flour,
50 g (1.75 oz) yeast,
200 g (7 oz) milk,
2 tablespoons sour cream,
100 g (3.5 oz) vegetable oil,
50 g (1.75 oz) sugar,
5 salt,
700 g (24.5 oz) apples.

For the crumbs:
150 g (5.25 oz) butter,
150 g (5.25 oz) sugar,
200 g (7 oz) flour,
vanillin or grated lemon zest

Prepare the dough with a starter. When the dough has risen, roll it out to a thickness of 1 cm (0.4 inches) and put it on a greased baking sheet. Peel and thinly slice the apples and arrange them in neat rows along the dough. Sprinkle the crumbs over the apples and bake in a medium oven for 25-30 minutes. To make the crumbs, mix together the flour, sugar and vanillin or lemon zest. Add the butter and process with your hands or with a pastry mixer until crumbs form.

Cottage cheese pastry

500 g (17.5 oz) flour,
250 g (8.75 oz) milk,
25 g (0.875 oz) yeast,
100 g (3.5 oz) butter,
100 g (3.5 oz) sugar,
2 eggs,
5 g (0.175 oz) salt,
1 egg

For the cottage cheese mixture:
750 g (26.25 oz) dry cottage cheese,
100 g (3.5 oz) sugar,
2 egg yolks,
50 g (1.75 oz) sour cream,
75 g (2.625 oz) raisins,
25 g (0.875 oz) flour,
the grated zest of 1 lemon

Prepare the dough without a starter. When the dough has risen, roll it out to a thickness of 1-1 1/2 cm (0.4-0.6 inches). Put it on a greased baking sheet, smooth it out and let it rise. Cover it with the cottage cheese mixture. Brush beaten egg over the mixture, and bake in a medium oven. Let the pastry cool and cut it into pieces.

For the cottage cheese mixture: Process or grind the cottage cheese and mix it together with all of the ingredients except the raisins. Rinse the raisins, drain them, roll them in the flour, and add them to the cottage cheese mixture last. Mix well.

Winter pastry

750 g (26.25 oz) flour,
25 g (0.875 oz) milk,
50 g (1.75 oz) yeast,
150 g (5.25 oz) butter,
100 g (3.5 oz) sugar,
2 eggs,
5 g (0.175 oz) salt,
25 g (0.875 oz) shelled almonds or hazelnuts,
1 egg,
powdered sugar

For the filling:
400 g (14 oz) sweet cream,
50 g (1.75 oz) sugar,
vanillin sugar

Prepare the dough with a starter. When the dough has risen, divide it into pieces of 45-50 g (1.4-1.575 oz). Use your hands to roll the dough into firm, round rolls. Place on a greased baking sheet and let them rise. Brush with beaten egg. Grind the nuts and sprinkle them over the rolls. Bake in a medium oven. When the rolls have puffed up, let them cool, and cut off their tops with a sharp knife. Whip the cream with the sugar and vanillin sugar. Fill the puffed rolls. Replace their tops and sprinkle the rolls with powdered sugar. You may replace grated nuts with a mixture of 1 tablespoon each of ice-cold butter, flour and sugar, pressed together into crumb-like mixture.

Tea bread

> 500 g (17.5 oz) flour;
> 200 g (7 oz) milk,
> 50 g (1.75 oz) yeast,
> 100 g (3.5 oz) butter,
> 100 g (3.5 oz) sugar;
> 2 egg yolks,
> 5 g (0.175 oz) salt

> For the nut mixture:
> 100 g (3.5 oz) nuts,
> 120 g (4.2 oz) sugar;
> 75 g (2.625 oz) butter,
> 25 g (0.875 oz) water

> For the cooked crème:
> 200 g (7 oz) milk,
> 75 g (2.625 oz) sugar;
> 2 eggs,
> 25 g (0.875 oz) flour;
> 150 g (5.25 oz) butter;
> vanillin sugar

Prepare the dough with a starter. When the dough has risen, roll it out to a thickness of 1-1 1/2 cm (0.4-0.6 inches), put it on a greased baking sheet, smooth it out and let it rise. Fold up the edges of the dough. Sprinkle the hot nut mixture over the surface of the dough, and bake at 230-240°C (446-464°F). Allow the pastry to cool and then cut it lengthwise to get 2 layers. Spread the cooked crème on top of one layer, add a second layer on top of it, and cut the pastry into pieces.

For the nut mixture: Boil the water, sugar and butter until the mixture is light yellow. Finely chop the nuts and add to the liquid. Continue cooking over a low flame until the mixture can be spread.

For the cooked crème: Put the flour on a dry pan and heat it until it is light yellow. Allow the flour to cool. Beat the eggs. Add the eggs to the flour. Boil the milk, sugar and vanillin and add in a thin stream into the flour and egg mixture. Mix well. Put the mixture on top of a double boiler, stirring, until thick. Remove the mixture from the heat. Cool it as quickly as possible. Add the butter and then whip the mixture with an electric beater or a whisk.

Boiled bacon rolls

> 250 g (8.75 oz) flour;
> 1/2 glass milk,
> 400 g (14 oz) butter;
> 25 g (0.875 oz) yeast,
> pinch of salt

> For the filling:
> 100 g (3.5 oz) dried bacon,
> 1 onion, black pepper

Put the milk, butter and salt in a pot and heat them to 30°C (86°F). Sprinkle the yeast into the mixture, along with the flour. Mix and knead until you get a medium-thick dough. Roll out the dough fairly thin. Use a cookie cutter to press out rounds. Put 1 teaspoon of the filling in the center of each round, press together the edges, and boil the rolls in salt water. Boil them for 5-8 minutes. Serve hot, with melted butter and sour cream. For the filling: Cut up the onion and sauté it for a bit. Cut up the bacon and add the onion, along with the pepper.

Pastry dough

1.2 kg (42 oz) flour,
500 g (17.5 oz) milk,
50 g (1.75 oz) yeast,
350 g (12.25 oz) butter (150 g (5.25 oz) for
*   the dough, 200 g (7 oz) to spread over the*
*   pastry),*
150 g (5.25 oz) sugar,
3 eggs + 1 egg, powdered sugar

Prepare the layered dough, roll it out and use it to prepare various pastries.

Rose pastries: Roll out the dough to a thickness of 1 1/2 cm (0.6 inches), cut it into squares 8 x 8 cm (3.2 x 3.2 inches), fold up the four corners of each square and press them together in the middle to create a blossom effect. Put the prepared pastries on a pastry board, pressed side down, and let them rise. Turn the pastries over, put them on a baking sheet, brush them with melted butter and bake.

Snail shells: Roll out the dough to a thickness of 1 cm (0.4 inches) and cut strips that are 1-1 1/2 cm (0.4-0.6 inches) wide and 25-30 cm (10-12 inches) long. Roll up each strip of dough from one end to form a shape similar to a snail's shell.

Twisted pastries: Roll out the dough, cut it into strips and twist it into various shapes.

Fruit pastries: Roll out the dough to a thickness of 1 cm and cut it into strips that are 10 cm (4 inches) wide. Spread your favorite fruit marmalade across 2/3 of the strips and then fold them up, starting with the end of the strip that does not have marmalade on it. Cut the folded strips into slices 3-3 1/2 cm (1.2-1.4 inches) wide.

Poppy seed pastries: Roll out the dough to a thickness of 0.8-1 cm (0.3-0.4 inches). Spread the poppy seed filling over dough, and roll it up into a roll 5-6 cm (2-2.4 inches) in diameter. Cut the roll into thick slices and place on a greased baking sheet, cut side down.

For the poppy seed filling: Rinse 250 g (8.75 oz) of poppy seeds several times. Put them in a bowl. Pour boiling water over seeds to cover. Set aside for 15-20 minutes, and drain. Grind the seeds in a food processor or using a mortar and pestle. Mix with 100 g (3.5 oz) sugar, 50 g (1.75 oz) honey and 2 egg yolks. You may also add raisins, chopped nuts or port wine to the mixture if you desire.

Cinnamon pastries: Prepare these just like the poppy seed pastries. Instead of the poppy seed filling, brush the pastry with melted butter and then sprinkle sugar mixed together with cinnamon across the surface.

Pastries with cottage cheese: Roll out the dough to a thickness of 1/2-1 cm (0.2-0.4 inches) and cut into squares that are 8 x 8 cm (3.2 x 3.2 inches) in size. Place a bit of sweetened cottage cheese filling in the center of each square and fold up the corners. Put the pastries on a greased baking sheet, let them rise, brush them with a beaten egg and bake at 220-230°C (428-446°F) for 10-15 minutes.

Many of these pastries can be sprinkled with chopped nuts or crumbs (see the second version of the recipe for apple pastry, above).

Holiday crown

800 g (28 oz) flour,
250 g (8.75 oz) milk,
75-100 g (3.5 oz) yeast,
250 g (8.75 oz) butter,
5 eggs, 200 g (7 oz) sugar,
the grated zest of 1 lemon,
5 cardamom seeds,
10 g (0.35 oz) salt,
1 egg, powdered sugar

To spread on the pastry:
200 g (7 oz) butter,
200 g (7 oz) sugar,
1 glass raisins,
1 teaspoon cinnamon

Mix the butter and the flour with a pastry blender or with two knives. Beat together the eggs and the sugar. Remove the husks from the cardamom seeds and grind the seeds in a spice grinder. Add the cardamom and the grated lemon zest to the butter and flour mixture. Warm the milk. Dissolve the yeast in it, add the salt, and the eggs, and then mix the yeast mixture together with the butter and flour. Let the dough rise. When the dough is risen, split it up into three portions, rolling each of them out to a thickness of 1/2-1 cm (0.2-0.4 inches). Whip together the sugar and the butter and spread it across each of the pieces of dough. Sprinkle each piece with raisins and cinnamon, and then roll the pieces up into a tight roll. Use all three rolls to weave a braid (start weaving from the middle). When you have the braid, shape it into a circle. Put it on a greased baking sheet, let it rise, brush it with beaten egg, and bake in a medium oven for approximately 50 minutes. Let the pastry cool a bit and then sprinkle it with powdered sugar before serving.

Latvian birthday cake (*kliņģeris*)

1 kg (2 lb, 3 oz) flour,
400 g (14 oz) milk,
75 g (2.625 oz) yeast,
350 g (12.25 oz) butter,
250 g (8.75 oz) sugar,
8 egg yolks,
200 g (7 oz) raisins,
the grated zest of 1 lemon,
1/2 g (0.0175 oz) saffron,
10 g (0.35 oz) salt,
50 g (1.75 oz) almonds or other nuts,
1 egg, powdered sugar

Prepare the dough with a starter. When the starter has risen, beat the butter with sugar and egg yolks and add it to the starter. Add the lemon peel and saffron. Rinse and drain the raisins. Roll them in flour, and add to the starter. Knead well and let rise. (The easiest way to add the saffron (especially with experience) is to crumble it between your fingers. Add a bit of warm milk or water. Let it sit until the saffron has yielded its color and flavor. Remove the saffron bits, and add the yellow liquid to the dough.) Roll the dough into a long "rope" and form it into the shape of a pretzel. Put it on a greased baking sheet and let it rise again. Brush beaten egg over the surface, sprinkle chopped almonds or other nuts on top, and bake. Sprinkle powdered sugar on the *kliņģeris* when it has cooled.

Apple pancakes

Thick egg pancakes

Potato pancakes

Thin pancakes stuffed with mushrooms

PANCAKES

Thin pancakes stuffed with cottage cheese

Thin pancakes stuffed with meat

Apple pastry

Cottage cheese cake with crumbs

Traditional Latvian ambrosia

Bacon rolls (*pīrāgi*), bouillon *pīrāgi*

DESSERTS, BREADS, PASTRY AND CAKES

Strawberries with milk

Whipped cream with baked apple

Sour cream jelly

Vanilla cream

Dried fruit cream

The elixir of a nation – "Riga Black Balsam"

The excellent herbal bitter is made with 24 ingredients which give its original appeal and charm. The original recipe dates back to the 18th century when pharmacist Kunce integrated the tastes and aromas of herbs, buds, flowers, oils and berries to create its unique formula.

The elixir is much more than the backbone of a nation. It is Latvia's most famous visit card. Presidents have received "Riga Black Balsam" as official gifts, and cities the world around have received the elixir from Latvian delegations.

Savour "Riga Black Balsam" pure or in cocktails and enjoy the tradition, mystery and delicious taste of a master's creation.

Yeast dough for *pīrāgi*

500 g (17.5 oz) flour,
300 g (10.5 oz) butter,
1/2 glass water,
50 g (1.75 oz) yeast,
1 teaspoon vinegar,
1/2 teaspoon salt,
1 egg

For the filling:
350 g (12.25 oz) fatty bacon,
1 onion,
pepper

Sift the dough onto a pastry board. Incorporate the butter with a pastry blender. Form a small "hill" with the flour and butter, with an indentation in the middle. Dissolve the yeast in the water, add the vinegar and salt to it, and pour the liquid into the flour. Use a knife to incorporate the liquid into the flour, and then use your hands to knead the mixture into a uniform dough. Refrigerate it for 30 minutes. Then roll the dough out very thin (5 mm) and cut it up into equal squares (a pizza cutter works well for this). Brush beaten egg across one corner of each square, and put some filling in the middle. Fold over the corner which does not have egg on it and press together the edges. Put the *pīrāgi* on a greased baking sheet, brush with beaten egg and bake in a hot oven. The filling is prepared as in the previous recipe. You can also fill these pastries with cooked ground beef.

Bacon rolls (*pīrāgi*)

450-500 g flour,
250 g (8.75 oz) milk,
25 g (0.875 oz) yeast,
75 g (2.625 oz) butter,
25 g (0.875 oz) sugar,
5 g (0.175 oz) salt,
1 egg

For the filling:
350 g (12.25 oz) fatty bacon,
50 g (1.75 oz) onion,
pepper

Prepare the dough with or without a starter. When the dough has risen, take small pieces of dough (30-35 g) and roll each out into a round. Let the rounds rise for 10-15 minutes. Press them down flat, put some of the bacon mixture in the middle of each one, and press together the edges. Use your hands to even out the filling in the middle of the pastry. Shape the pastries into half-moon shapes and put them on a greased baking sheet. Let them rise again, brush them with beaten egg, and bake them in a hot oven. When the *pīrāgi* are done, brush them with melted butter.

For the filling: Cut the bacon into small pieces and chop the onion. Sauté. (The fat in the bacon helps the filling to hold together). Sprinkle with pepper and mix well. The onions are optional but add delicious flavor.

Bouillon *pīrāgi*

3 glasses flour,
1 glass milk,
250 g (8.75 oz) butter,
50 g (1.75 oz) yeast,
1 tablespoon sugar,
1/2 teaspoon salt,
2-3 eggs

For the filling:
600-700 g cooked beef,
1-2 onions,
1 tablespoon butter,
salt, pepper,
beef stock

Warm the milk, add the salt, sugar and yeast, and stir until the yeast is dissolved. Sift the flour and add it to the mixture. Mix well. Melt the butter and add it to the dough. Knead the dough well and refrigerate it for 1-2 hours. Roll the dough out, roll it up and divide into 6 or 7 portions. Roll out each portion into a round that is 5 mm thick. Use a pizza cutter to cut out 12 tri-angles. Put some filling on the wide edge of each triangle. Roll up the triangles into rolls and press down the edges. Put the pastries on a greased baking sheet, brush with beaten egg and bake in a hot oven.

For the filling: Grind the beef with some chopped onion that you have sautéed in butter. Add the beef stock, salt and pepper and heat.

Summer *pīrāgi*

2 glasses flour,
200 g (7 oz) butter,
2 tablespoons sour cream,
salt,
1 egg

For the filling:
3 hard-boiled eggs,
100-150 g (3.5-5.25 oz) green onion,
60 g (2.1 oz) butter,
1/2 teaspoon salt

Cut the butter into the flour with a knife or pastry blender and add the sour cream and salt. Use your hands to knead the mixture into a uniform dough. Refrigerate the dough for 1 hour. Then roll out the dough very thin (3 mm in thickness). Use a cookie cutter to cut out rounds. Place some filling in the middle of each round, fold over and press together the edges. Shape the folded rounds into half-moon shapes and put them on a greased baking sheet. Brush them with beaten egg and bake them in a hot oven.

For the filling: Beat the butter and finely dice the green onion and hard-boiled eggs. Mix together all of the ingredients.

Cottage cheese cake with crumbs (serves 8-16)

125 g (4.375 oz) dry cottage cheese,
5 tablespoons vegetable oil,
5 tablespoons milk,
65 g (2.275 oz) sugar,
250 g (8.75 oz) flour,
1 teaspoon baking powder or 1/2 teaspoon each
*   of drinking soda and lemon juice*

For the filling:
2 glasses milk, 4 eggs,
1 glass sugar,
2 tablespoons flour,
vanillin,
100 g (3.5 oz) dry cottage cheese,
200 g (7 oz) dried fruit

For the crumbs:
100 g (3.5 oz) flour,
75 g (2.625 oz) butter,
30 g (1.05 oz) sugar,
vanillin

Make sure that you have dry cottage cheese, or this will not work. Grind the cottage cheese, add the milk, oil and sugar, and mix well. Add half of the flour and beat the mixture for 2 minutes. Sift the remaining flour with the baking powder and add it into the mixture with your hands. Roll out the dough. Grease a baking sheet and lay the dough into it, leaving 4 cm (1.6 inches) of overhang on all sides. Fold up the overhang to create edges for the pastry. Spread the filling all across the surface of the dough, sprinkle the crumbs across the filling, and bake the pastry in a medium oven for approximately 45 minutes.

For the filling: Beat together the eggs and the sugar, add the flour and vanillin, stir well and set aside. Heat the milk to a bit less than the boiling point and add it to the egg and sugar mixture, stirring all the while. Put the mixture back into the pot and, stirring constantly, heat it up until it thickens. Let the mixture cool. While it is cooling, grind the cottage cheese. Add it and the dried fruit (if you use raisins, put them in whole, but if you are using dried apricots or apples, chop up the pieces first) to the other ingredients.

For the crumbs: Mix together the flour, sugar and vanillin. Add the butter (this is easier if it is ice-cold) and cut it with a pastry blender or two knives until you get crumbs.

You may replace the filling with sliced plums or apples if you like.

Oatmeal cookies

500 g (17.5 oz) oatmeal (not instant),
250 g (8.75 oz) butter,
200 g (7 oz) sugar, 3 eggs,
the grated zest of 1 lemon

Shake the oats in a sifter over a bowl. Toast the oats in the butter for a bit and then let them cool. Beat together the sugar and the butter. Add them to the oats. Add the lemon zest and the eggs, along with the oat scraps that fell into the bowl when you sifted the oats. Mix thoroughly. Use a teaspoon to spoon the dough on a greased baking sheet. Bake until golden. Let the cookies cool. Remove them from the baking sheet with a spatula. These cookies are very fragile.

Hard gingerbread

350 g (12.25 oz) syrup and honey,
150 g (5.25 oz) butter,
200 g (7 oz) sugar, 2 eggs,
2 g (0.07 oz) baking soda,
600 g (21 oz) flour,
spices (see below),
1 egg

Bring the syrup, honey, butter and sugar to a boil, stirring all the while to avoid burning. While the mixture is still boiling, add one-half of the flour, along with all of the spices, and keep stirring until the dough is uniform and is starting to peel away from the sides of the pot. Let the dough cool a bit. Beat the eggs and dissolve the baking soda in some water. Add the eggs, the soda and the rest of the flour to the dough and mix well. Place onto a pastry board or counter-top and knead it until it is smooth and shiny. This will take some work. Roll out the dough thinly and use various cookie cutters to cut out shapes. Put the cookies on an ungreased baking sheet. Brush with beaten egg. Sprinkle them with chopped hazelnuts or almonds, and bake.

For the spices:
1/2 teaspoon cinnamon,
10 cloves,
5 cardamom seeds,
1/2 teaspoon ground nutmeg,
1 teaspoon ginger,
1 teaspoon ground coriander,
5 peppercorns.

Grind together all of the spices until you get a fine powder.

Children's cookies

160 g (5.6 oz) flour,
200 g (7 oz) potato starch,
100 g (3.5 oz) butter,
100-150 g (3.5-5.25 oz) sugar,
2 egg yolks,
120 g (4.2 oz) sour cream,
the grated zest and juice of 1/2 lemon,
1 teaspoon baking powder,
glaze (see below),
candied fruit for decoration

Beat together the butter and sugar and then add the egg yolks, one by one, along with the cream, the lemon zest, the lemon juice, the potato starch, the baking powder and the flour. Work the mixture quickly with a mixer or your hands to form a uniform dough. Roll out the dough to a thickness of 5 mm. Use various cookie cutters to cut out shapes. Put them on a greased baking sheet and bake in a moderate oven until they are golden. Let the cookies cool, then glaze them and decorate them with candied fruit or colored sugar.

For an egg glaze: Whip 1 egg white, gradually adding 150 g (5.25 oz) of powdered sugar and a bit of lemon juice.

For a chocolate glaze: Boil together 100 g (3.5 oz) sugar with 4 tablespoons of simple syrup, add 1 tablespoon of powdered cocoa and 1 tablespoon of melted butter.

Soft gingerbread

400 g (14 oz) syrup and honey,
100 g (3.5 oz) sugar,
100 g (3.5 oz) butter,
2 eggs,
400 g (14 oz) flour,
25 g (0.875 oz) yeast,
spices (as in the previous recipe),
1 egg, nuts

Bring the syrup, honey, butter and sugar to a boil, stirring all the while to avoid burning. While the mixture is still boiling, add most of the flour, along with all of the spices, and beat thoroughly. Let the mixture cool a bit. Beat the eggs and dissolve the yeast in some water. Add the eggs, yeast and the rest of the flour and mix well. Pour the dough onto a greased baking sheet at a thickness of 1-1 1/2 cm (0.2-0.4 inches). Let it rise for a bit. Brush with beaten egg. Sprinkle with chopped nuts. Bake in a medium oven. Let the gingerbread cool and cut it into squares.

Alexander cake

320 g flour,
100 g (3.5 oz) sugar,
100 g (3.5 oz) margarine,
1 egg,
150 g (5.25 oz) sugar,
1/2 teaspoon cinnamon,
1 teaspoon baking powder

For the filling:
1/2 glass raspberry jam

For the glaze:
The juice of 1/2 lemon,
100 g (3.5 oz) powdered sugar

Whip butter and margarine with sugar. Add the egg. Mix the flour with the baking powder and cinnamon. Add to the butter mixture, and mix thoroughly. Refrigerate the cake dough for 1 hour. Roll the dough out to a thickness of 5 mm, put it on a baking sheet and bake for 20-25 minutes. Cut the pastry in half. Spread the jam on one half, put the other half on top and press lightly. Spread the glaze over the cake. (Mix together the lemon juice and powdered sugar until thick.) Spread while the cake is still warm. Cut the cake into squares.

"Twigs"

2 eggs,
75 g (2.625 oz) sugar,
150 g (5.25 oz) sour cream,
500 g (17.5 oz) flour,
1 g (0.035 oz) baking soda,
20 g (0.7 oz) vodka, vanillin, salt,
vegetable oil for deep frying, powdered sugar

Whip the eggs with sugar and vanillin. Add sour cream, baking soda, vodka, salt and flour, and knead well. Roll out the dough into a thin layer and cut it into lengths 10 cm (4 inches) long and 4-5 cm (1.6-2 inches) wide. Use a ridged pizza or cookie cutter to cut off one edge of the strips for a decorative effect, and then roll up the strips lengthwise. Fry the cookies in oil until they are golden in colour. Cool. Sprinkle with powdered sugar.

121

Apples in layered butter dough

300 g (10.5 oz) flour;
200 g (7 oz) butter;
125 g (4.375 oz) water;
1/2 egg,
1/2 g (0.0175 oz) lemon juice,
salt,
1 egg,
powdered sugar

Filling:
Approximately 1 kg (2 lb, 3 oz) medium-tart
   apple, sugar, cinnamon

Put the water in a large bowl. Add the lemon juice, salt, egg and 200 g (7 oz) of the flour. Stir and knead until the dough no longer sticks to the sides of the bowl. Add the butter into the remaining 100 g (3.5 oz) of flour. Shape the mixture into a flat rectangle and refrigerate it. Roll out the dough so that you get a rectangle, rolling the sides of the dough somewhat more thinly than the center. Put the butter mixture in the middle of the dough, fold over the edges, press lightly, and then carefully roll out again to a thickness of 1 1/2 cm (0.6 inches). Fold up the edges and then fold the pastry in half. Cover it with a damp cloth and refrigerate for 20-30 minutes. Repeat the procedure two more times, folding the dough into thirds last time and refrigerating it again. While the dough is refrigerating, peel and core the whole apples, keeping them intact. When the dough is cold, roll it out to a thickness of approximately 3 mm and cut it up into large squares. In the center of each square of dough, place one of the apples. Sprinkle sugar and cinnamon inside the apple and fold up the corners of the dough, pressing together at the top to cover the apple completely. Brush with beaten egg. Place on a greased baking sheet and bake at 250-260°C (482-500°F). When the pastries have cooled, sprinkle them with powdered sugar.

Quick dough: Freeze the butter and then incorporate it into the flour until the mixture resembles crumbs. Into the center of the crumby mixture, add the water (in which you first dissolved salt and lemon juice). Add the egg and then quickly knead the dough until it is uniform. Refrigerate it for 2-3 hours before proceeding as directed above.

Caraway bread sticks

150 g (5.25 oz) flour;
150 g (5.25 oz) boiled potato;
150 g (5.25 oz) butter;
1/2 teaspoon salt,
1 egg,
caraway seeds

Process or grind the potatoes. Mix together the flour and the salt. Add the flour mixture to the potatoes and then add butter. Knead the mixture until you have a uniform dough. Refrigerate it for 30 minutes. Roll out the dough and cut out sticks 12-15 cm (4.8-6 inches) long and 1 cm (0.4 inches) wide. Put the sticks on a greased baking sheet. Brush them with beaten egg, and sprinkle with caraway seeds. Bake in a medium oven until golden. Let the caraway sticks cool. Arrange by standing them up in a dish.

Biscuit torte

8 eggs,
160 g (5.6 oz) sugar,
120 g (4.2 oz) flour,
50 g (1.75 oz) potato starch,
spices,
1 teaspoon baking powder

For the filling:
0.75 liters sweet cream,
70 g (2.45 oz) sugar,
vanillin,
3-4 medium-tart apples,
200 g (7 oz) cranberry jelly,
100 g (3.5 oz) ground or sliced hazelnuts

Biscuit cake dough (hot method): Put all of the eggs, sugar and the spices (according to your own taste) in a large, preferably a heat-resistant ceramic bowl. Put the bowl on top of a pot of simmering water and heat, stirring constantly, to a temperature of 40°C (104°F). Keep stirring until the mixture is light in color and has tripled or quadrupled in volume. Remove the bowl from the hot water, and keep whipping the mixture until it cools to lukewarm. Mix together the flour and the potato starch and add them gradually to the egg mixture. Add the baking powder. Pour the dough into a pan which is lined with baking paper and bake at 200-220°C (392-428°F) for approximately 30 minutes, until the biscuit is golden and starts to pull away from the sides of the pan. When a toothpick inserted into the center of the dough and comes out clean, it is ready. Let the biscuit cool thoroughly and then cut it horizontally into two layers. Spread sweetened whipped cream across one layer. Put the other layer on top of it, and again spread with the whipped cream. Add vanilla to the sweetened whipped cream for additional flavor. Peel and slice the apples and blanch in sugar water. Lay the slices neatly across the top of the torte. Spread whipped cream along the sides of the torte to cover. Apply hazelnuts to the sides of the torte. Use a pastry bag to decorate the top of the torte with whipped cream. Finally, spread the cranberry jelly on top of the apple slices.

Variations: Use your imagination to fill this torte. Add sliced strawberries to the whipped cream, for example, and decorate the torte with sliced strawberries. You can also fill the torte with vanilla cream and strawberry jam. The torte can also be cut into three slices and filled with jam and chocolate cream (see below).

Chocolate cream:
200 g (7 oz) sugar,
100 g (3.5 oz) water,
3 eggs,
400 g (14 oz) butter,
50 g (1.75 oz) cocoa powder,
25 g (0.875 oz) cognac

Boil the sugar and water into a syrup. Beat the eggs and very slowly add the syrup to them, beating the mixture continuously. Continue whipping the mixture until it has cooled. Add the cocoa and mix. Whip the butter and gradually add it into the egg mixture along with the cognac.

Cottage cheese torte

4 egg yolks, 6 egg whites,
4 tablespoons sugar,
4 tablespoons wheat flour, vanillin

For the cottage cheese mixture:
350 g dry cottage cheese,
200 g (7 oz) butter,
1 glass powdered sugar,
2 egg yolks, 1 glass sweet cream,
2 tablespoons chopped candied orange peel,
1/2 lemon, 1/2 glass milk,
20 g (0.7 oz) gelatin

Preparing the cake dough (cold method): Separate the eggs carefully. Beat the egg yolks, gradually adding approximately 3/4 of the sugar, along with spices according to your own taste. Beat the mixture until the sugar has dissolved and the mixture is light and airy. Whip the egg whites separately to firm peaks. Add part of the egg whites to the yolks. Mix together the flour and the potato starch and gradually add them to the egg mixture, stirring continously. Finally, add the remaining whipped egg whites. (Do not beat the mixture excessively. The egg whites will lose their volume.) Put the dough in a round cake pan which is lined with baking paper and bake at 200-220°C (392-428°F) for approximately 30 minutes, until the biscuit is golden and starts to pull away from the sides of the pan. It is ready when a toothpick is inserted into dough and comes out clean.

For the filling: Whip together the butter and the powdered sugar. Add the egg yolks and mix thoroughly. Grate the cottage cheese. Peel the lemon and grate its zest. Add the cottage cheese and the lemon zest to the egg mixture, along with the grated candied orange peel. Heat the gelatin in the milk to saturate it and then add it to the egg mixture, too. Whip the cream and incorporate it into the mixture.

For decoration: *3/4 glass berry juice (any kind), 1/3 glass water, sugar, 10 g gelatin.* Saturate the gelatin in the water. Heat the berry juice with the sugar. Add the gelatin mixture and refrigerate until slightly thickened.

To prepare the cake: When the biscuit round has cooled thoroughly, cover it completely with the cottage cheese mixture on the top and the sides. Even out the surface and the edges and refrigerate until the mixture hardens. Then decorate the surface of the cake with slices of orange or strawberries. Pour the gelatin mixture all across the cake. Refrigerate the cake until the gelatin is firm.

Cottage cheese cake

250 g (8.75 oz) butter,
300 g (10.5 oz) dry cottage cheese,
250 g (8.75 oz) sugar,
500 g (17.5 oz) flour, 4 eggs,
1/2 glass raisins,
the grated zest and juice of 1 lemon,
1 teaspoon baking powder, salt

Whip sugar, and add the eggs one by one. Process or grind the cottage cheese and sift the flour together with the baking powder. Mix together all of the ingredients. Pour the dough into a Bundt pan, and bake in a medium oven for approximately 50 minutes. Sprinkle with powdered sugar before serving.

Līgo torte

For the cake dough:
300 g (10.5 oz) flour;
200 g (7 oz) butter;
100 g (3.5 oz) sugar;
1 egg, vanillin

Beat together the butter and sugar. Add the egg and the vanillin. Sift in the flour, mix well and refrigerate for 30 minutes.

For the cottage cheese mixture:
300 g (10.5 oz) dry cottage cheese,
200 g (7 oz) rhubarb, 2 eggs,
75 g (2.625 oz) sugar;
20 g (0.7 oz) manna-croup,
20 g (0.7 oz) flour;
1/2 glass candied orange peel,
vanillin

Beat together the eggs and sugar. Process or grind the cottage cheese and add it to the mixture. Peel and finely dice the rhubarb and chop the candied orange peel. Add all of the ingredients to the cottage cheese mixture and mix well.

For the biscuit cake dough:
3 eggs,
60 g (2.1 oz) sugar;
60 g (2.1 oz) flour, vanillin

Prepare the biscuit cake dough according to the cold method. To assemble the torte, do the following:

Take 12 small, round cookie cutters and put them on a baking sheet. Fill with some of the first dough into each, and bake until you have 12 small cookies. Roll out the rest of the dough. Lay it in a round pan and bake in a moderate oven for approximately 20 minutes. Spread the cottage cheese mixture over the dough in the round baking pan and bake for another 20 minutes.

Use some of the biscuit dough to bake six small, round cookies. Pour the rest of the cake dough over the cottage cheese mixture and put the pan back in the oven until the biscuit is baked through.

Let the torte cool. Spread the rhubarb mixture all over it. Dip the first cookies in cranberry juice and then roll them in sugar. Use them to decorate the sides of the cake. Roll the biscuit cookies into small "purses", and arrange them in the shape of a flower blossom in the center of the torte.

Anna's torte

200 g (7 oz) butter;
200 g (7 oz) sugar;
4-5 eggs,
the grated zest and juice of 1/2 lemon,
250 g (8.75 oz) flour;
6 tablespoons raisins

Beat butter with sugar. Separate the eggs and add the yolks one by one to the mixture. Add the lemon zest and juice. Sift the flour over the raisins. Mix them together, and add to the mixture. Whip the egg whites and add them to the mixture. Grease a cake pan, pour the cake dough into it, and bake at a moderate temperature for approximately 40 minutes. When the cake has cooled, remove it from the pan and sprinkle it with powdered sugar.

Apple cake

250 g (8.75 oz) flour,
150 g (5.25 oz) butter, 1/2 egg,
100 g (3.5 oz) water, 1/2 g lemon juice,
1 egg for brushing

For the filling:
1 kg (2 lb, 3 oz) medium-tart apple,
200 g (7 oz) sugar, cinnamon

For the apple mixture: Peel, core and dice the apples. Put them in a pot with a bit of water, add the sugar, and bring to a boil. Add the cinnamon. The apples can be replaced with rhubarb, or you can use vanilla cream to fill the pastry instead of the apples.

Prepare layered pastry dough. Roll it out to a thickness of 1/2-1 cm (0.2-0.4 inches), enough to cover your baking sheet. (Place dough on baking sheet.) Use a knife to score the dough in diamond shapes (not cutting through), and then press with a fork to poke holes into the middle of each of the diamonds. Brush beaten egg over the surface of the dough and bake in a hot oven until golden. (When the pastry is ready, its edges should break off easily.) Cool the pastry and then cut it in half. Spread the apple mixture over one half of the pastry, put the other half of the pastry on top and press lightly. Use a very sharp knife to cut up the cake into serving pieces.

Honey torte

3 glasses flour, 2 eggs,
100 g (3.5 oz) butter,
1 glass sugar, 1 tablespoon honey,
1 teaspoon baking soda

For the filling:
1 glass jam (strawberry or cranberry),
2 glasses sour cream, 1 glass sugar,
the grated zest of 1 lemon

For decorating:
1 glass oatmeal (not instant),
1 tablespoon sugar,
1 tablespoon butter,
slices of red and green marmalade

Put the eggs and sugar into a pot. Cut the butter into pieces and add it to the pot. Heat, stirring constantly, until the sugar melts. In a separate pot, heat the honey and the baking soda, stirring all the while, until the honey is foamy and brown, and the foam settles. Mix together the contents of both pots, adding the flour. Mix to get a uniform dough. Divide the dough into six parts, and roll each part out into a round of equal size, at a thickness of 3-5 mm. Poke holes in each round with a fork and bake each one individually in a medium oven for 5-10 minutes. While the cakes are still warm, stack them, putting jam and sour cream mixture between the layers. Cut around the cake with a sharp knife to even out the edges. Spread sour cream mixture over the top and sides of the torte. Toast the oats in some butter. Let them cool and mix them with a tablespoon of sugar. Sprinkle outs across the sides and edges of the torte. Decorate the top of the cake with slices of marmalade.

For the sour cream mixture: 6-8 hours before baking the cake, whip sour cream with sugar and lemon zest. Refrigerate until needed.

Fill honey torte with vanilla cream, allowing the cake to cool a bit before you fill it.

Christmas torte

> *200 g (7 oz) butter, 4 eggs,*
> *300 g (10.5 oz) hard gingerbread,*
> *1 glass chopped walnuts,*
> *1/2 glass sugar, 1/2 glass milk,*
> *1 teaspoon baking powder,*
> *Black Balsam or rum*

> For the cream:
> *1 glass sugar,*
> *1/2 glass water, 3 eggs,*
> *400 g (14 oz) butter,*
> *50 g (1.75 oz) cocoa, 2 tablespoons cognac*

> For the filling: *1 glass jam*

> To cover the sides of the torte: *Grated gin-*
> *gerbread and chopped hard candies*

Whip the butter with sugar, and add the egg yolks one at a time. Finely grate the gingerbread, and add it to the sugar mixture along with milk, chopped nuts and baking powder. Mix the egg whites with 2 tablespoons of sugar. Beat into peaks and mix into the gingerbread mixture. Bake the torte in a cake pan in a medium oven. Allow the torte to cool and cut it horizontally into three large rounds. Use a sharp knife to trim the edges of the three rounds and cut up the scraps. Set them aside. Sprinkle some Balsam or rum over each of the rounds. Spread most of the darker portion of the cream (see below) on one of the rounds, put the second round on top of it, spread the jam over the second round, and put the third round on top. Cover the top and the sides of the torte with the lighter cream and then sprinkle the grated gingerbread and hard candies all across the top and sides of the cake. Sprinkle the chopped scraps from the sides of the cake on top, and use a pastry bag to decorate the cake with more of the darker cream. Sprinkle powdered sugar over the surface.

For the cream: Boil the sugar and water into a syrup. Let it cool. Beat the eggs. While the syrup is still warm, add it to the eggs. Let the mixture cool. Whip the butter. Add the egg mixture to it and beat, adding the cognac gradually. Divide the cream into two parts. Mix more cocoa into one part and less in the other to form a lighter and a darker cream.

Rye bread torte

> *8 eggs,*
> *150 g (5.25 oz) dry rye bread,*
> *160 g (5.6 oz) sugar,*
> *1 teaspoon cinnamon*

> For the filling:
> *1 1/2 glasses loganberry jam,*
> *3 glasses sweet cream,*
> *80 g (2.8 oz) sugar, vanillin*

Grate the dry rye bread into fine crumbs. Prepare the biscuit cake dough as directed above, substituting the rye bread crumbs and the cinnamon for the flour in the recipe. Bake as directed, cool thoroughly and split into two layers. Whip the cream until it is quite firm. Spread the jam over one of the layers and then spread whipped cream across the jam to cover. Put the other layer of the torte on top and spread it lightly with the jam. Then cover the top and the sides of the cake completely with whipped cream. Decorate the cake with the last of the whipped cream and stewed fruit.

The Rēzekne torte

500 g (17.5 oz) flour,
300 g (10.5 oz) butter,
150 g (5.25 oz) sugar,
2 eggs,
the grated zest of 1 lemon

For the cream:
1 jar sweetened condensed milk,
400 g (14 oz) butter,
2 tablespoons cognac,
vanilla extract

For the filling:
1 kg (2 lb, 3 oz) medium-tart apples,
the grated zest of 1 lemon

For decorating:
1 glass cranberry jelly,
1 glass sweet cream,
1 tablespoon sugar,
1 packet vanilla sugar

For the cake dough: Mix together flour and sugar, along with the grated lemon zest. Incorporate the butter into the flour with a pastry blender or a knife. Beat the eggs and add them to the mixture and keep blending or chopping until the dough starts to hold together. Knead it quickly to produce a uniform dough and refrigerate it for one hour.

Put the dough through a meat grinder, spread the pieces all across a baking sheet and bake them in the oven, stirring occasionally, until they are browned. Let them cool completely and then mix them into the cream.

For the cream: Beat butter gradually adding sweetened condensed milk. Keep whipping, adding the vanilla extract and cognac.

Peel and core the apples and cut into 4-6 pieces. Put them on a baking sheet with edges. Add 3/4 glass of water, sprinkle with 1 tablespoon sugar, and sauté in the oven until soft. (Do not let them get mushy.)

For the jelly: Add 1 glass of boiling water to 1/3 glass cranberry juice, along with 1-2 tablespoons of sugar and 2 teaspoons of gelatin. Let the mixture set.

To shape the torte: Put half of the cream mixture on a plate and mold it into a round "cake". Arrange the apple pieces on top, and then sprinkle with grated lemon zest. Put the remaining mixture on top. Use a teaspoon to make seven indentations along the edges of the torte and one indentation on top. Put some of the thickened cranberry jelly into each of these indentations. Beat cream with sugar and the vanilla sugar. Use a pastry bag to squeeze the whipped cream around the cranberry "lakes".

Mother's torte

2 glasses sour cream,
4 glasses flour,
salt

For the cream:
500 g (17.5 oz) butter,
2 1/2 glasses powdered sugar,
4 eggs,
vanillin,
25 g (0.875 oz) cognac

Mix the flour, a pinch of salt and sour cream together. Stir and knead until you get a dough. Refrigerate for 1 hour. Roll out pieces of the dough into 14 thin rounds of equal size. Bake them in a moderate oven until they are golden.

Let the rounds cool, then stack them, putting some of the cream in between each two layers and pressing down a bit. Cut all around the cake with a sharp knife to even out the edges. Crumble up the pieces of pastry that you have cut off and sprinkle them across the top of the torte. Spread the remaining cream all around the sides of the cake.

For the cream: Whip together the butter and the powdered sugar. Add the eggs one by one, and then add the vanillin and cognac. Double or triple the recipe to make it much higher. It makes a nice wedding cake!

SWEET SAUCES, SYRUPS AND CANDY

These syrups can be used to make various refreshing beverages, or they can be served with creams, berries and ice cream. Sweet cream syrup is particularly nice with ice cream.

Black currant syrup

1 kg (2 lb, 3 oz) black currants,
1 l (1 quart + 4 tablespoons) water,
40 g (1.4 oz) lemon juice,
sugar

Mix the lemon juice with the water and bring to a boil. Crush the berries. When the water has boiled, let it cool somewhat and then pour it over the berries. Set aside for 24 hours. Put two layers of cheesecloth over a large bowl. Dump the berries and liquid into the cheesecloth. Twist and press to extract as much liquid as possible. Add as much sugar as there is juice. Stir with a wooden spoon until the sugar dissolves. The syrup can be used as a sauce for creams, ice creams and other desserts. It can also be used to make various refreshing beverages. You can prepare raspberry, cherry, strawberry, gooseberry and other berry syrups in the same way.

Cranberry sauce

200 g (7 oz) water,
50 g (1.75 oz) cranberries,
30 g (1.05 oz) sugar,
6 g (0.21 oz) potato starch

Rinse and crush the cranberries to extract their juice. Put the solids in a pot, cover them with water, boil and strain, reserving the liquid. Discard the berry solids. Add sugar and the potato starch (dissolve it in some water first) to the liquid. Bring the mixture to a boil. Remove from the heat and add the cranberry juice. You can prepare sauces from red currants, black currants, strawberries and other berries in the same way.

Vanilla sauce

200 g (7 oz) milk, 1 egg yolk,
30 g (1.05 oz) sugar, vanillin

Beat together the egg yolk, sugar and vanillin. Boil the milk and then add it to the egg mixture little by little, stirring constantly. Put the bowl in a hot water bath, stirring constantly, until sauce thickens.

Chocolate sauce

150 g (5.25 oz) milk,
40 g (1.4 oz) sugar,
10 g (0.35 oz) cocoa,
1/2 egg yolk,
4 g (0.14 oz) flour

Beat egg yolk and sugar. Add the cocoa and flour. Boil milk and add it to the egg mixture bit by bit, stirring constantly. Put the bowl in a hot water bath and heat, stirring constantly, until it thickens.

Dandelion syrup

500 g (17.5 oz) dandelion blossoms,
1 to 1 1/2 l (approximately 1 1/2 quart)
    water,
2 kg (4 lb, 6 oz) sugar,
2 teaspoons lemon juice

Pick the dandelion blossoms on a sunny day, around noon. Pour the water over the blossoms. Put them in a pot, cover and boil over a low flame for 10 minutes. Set aside for 12 hours. Strain, reserving the liquid. Discard the flowers. Add the sugar to the liquid and simmer over a low flame for 1 hour. Add the lemon juice at the end of the process. Fill into clean bottles and seal.

Jasmine syrup

1 kg (2 lb, 3 oz) jasmine blossoms,
1 l (1 quart + 4 tablespoons) water,
20 g (0.7 oz) lemon juice

Pick the jasmine blossoms when they are at the peak of their bloom. Boil the water with the lemon juice. Let it cool and pour it over the blossoms. Set aside for 24 hours. Strain, reserving the liquid. For each glass of liquid, add 1/2 glass sugar. Boil 6-8 minutes. The syrup should be light green and have a taste similar to wild strawberries. If you boil syrup for a while longer, it will turn brown and taste like malt extract. You can use that for gingerbread dough.

Ashberry syrup

500 g (17.5 oz) ashberries,
600 g (21 oz) sugar, 500 g (17.5 oz) water

Rinse the berries and pour hot water over them (1 l (1 quart + 4 tablespoons) of water for every liter of berries). Boil the mixture for 5 minutes. Strain, reserving the solids but discarding the water. Put the berries through a sieve to collect their juice. Boil the sugar and the water. Add the juice and bring to a boil again. Let the mixture cool and fill it into bottles.

131

Chokeberry syrup

1 kg (2 lb, 3 oz) chokeberries,
2 l (approximately 2 quarts) water,
2 tablespoons lemon juice,
1 1/2 kg (3.2 lb) sugar,
3 handfuls cherry leaves

Add the cherry leaves to the water and boil for 4-5 minutes. Strain, reserving the liquid. Add to the liquid 1/2 kg of sugar. Bring the liquid to a boil. Add 1 tablespoon of lemon juice. While the liquid is still boiling, pour it over the berries. Set aside for 24 hours. Strain and discard the solids. Add 1 kg (2 lb, 3 oz) sugar and 1 table-spoon lemon juice to the liquid and simmer for 30 minutes.

Quince syrup

First version: Halve and seed 1 kg (2 lb, 3 oz) of quince with a stainless steel knife. Cut off the hard layer from the fruit and slice the remaining fruit into thin slices. Put the slices in a dish, layering them with 750 g (26.25 oz) sugar. Cover and set aside for 10-12 hours, until the sugar has dissolved. Strain the juice, reserving the solids and the sweetened juice. Pour 250 g (8.75 oz) boiling water over the fruit and set it aside for 24 hours. Strain, reserving the liquid (you can use the fruit itself to make fruit compotes). Add the sweetened juice and bring to a boil. Fill into bottles, seal and keep in the refrigerator.

Second version: Use a stainless steel knife to cut thin slices from the fruit all the way to the core (1 kg (2 lb, 3 oz) of quince in all). Layer the sliced fruit and between 1 and 1 1/2 kg

of sugar in a dish. Refrigerate for 48 hours. Pour off the syrup that has accumulated in the dish, straining it through two layers of cheesecloth. Boil this syrup for 3-5 minutes, skimming off the foam as necessary. Pour water over the fruit solids to cover and bring the water to a boil. Simmer the fruit until it is tender. Add sugar and simmer for another 10 minutes. The sweet and thick quince sauce can be used to fill cakes and tortes or to make whipped desserts.

Sweet cream syrup

1 glass sweet cream, 1 glass sugar,
1/2 glass water,
30 g (1.05 oz) cognac, vanillin

Boil the sugar, water and vanillin into a syrup. Add the cream while it is still hot, and then add the cognac. Mix well. Fill into bottles.

Milk candy (penuche)

1 glass milk or sweet cream,
1 glass sugar, vanillin, 1 tablespoon butter,
extra butter to spread on baking paper

Bring milk or cream to a boil with the sugar and the vanillin. Add the butter, stirring constantly. Heat until the syrup becomes thick. The mixture must be thick and light brown. Spread butter across a piece of baking paper or on a plate and pour the mixture at a thickness of 1 cm (0.4 inches). Let it cool thoroughly. Cut into bite-sized pieces. You may add 100 g (3.5 oz) of toasted and ground nuts to the syrup.

Cranberries in syrup

First version: Choose large and ripe cranberries for this dish. Combine 1 glass sugar and 1 glass water and boil them into a simple syrup. Put the berries in the syrup and heat them for five minutes. Put them in a sieve, drain excess syrup, and roll cranberries thoroughly in powdered sugar.

Second version: Beat 1 egg white and 1 tablespoon of water until the egg white is foamy. Add 1/2 kg (17.5 oz) cranberries to the mixture. Put the berries into a sieve to drain off the excess egg white, and then roll them in 1/2 kg (17.5 oz) of powdered sugar (with flavorings of your own choice: vanillin, ginger, instant coffee or cocoa powder).

Pea pods in syrup

1 kg (2 lb, 3 oz) sugar,
2 1/2glasses water, 2 teaspoons lemon juice,
500 g (17.5 oz) pea pods

You need very young pea pods for this dish — in which the peas themselves have not yet begun to form. Clean the pods and open them up, getting two halves. Sauté them in a bit of water for 10-15 minutes. Combine the sugar and water and boil them into a simple syrup. Pour the syrup over the pea pods. Set aside for 12 hours. Drain the syrup into a pot. Bring it to a boil and let it cool. Pour it over the pea pods. Repeat this process three or four times. The last time, add the lemon juice to the syrup. Store the pea pods in jars in the refrigerator and use them to decorate cakes.

Pastille

First version:
2 kg (4 lb, 6 oz) berries,
1 kg (2 lb, 3 oz) sugar,
1/2 glass water,
powdered sugar

Boil the berries in the water and put them through a sieve. Combine the berry pulp with the sugar and cook over a slow flame until it thickens entirely. Pour the mixture on baking paper at a thickness of 1 cm (0.4 inches). When it has cooled, cut it into pieces and roll in powdered sugar. Pack into a cardboard box. Put baking paper between the layers. Use the pastille as candy, or to decorate cakes and tortes.

Second version:
2 kg (4 lb, 6 oz) apples,
1 kg (2 lb, 3 oz) sugar, 4 egg whites

Bake the apples and then put them through a sieve. In a mixer, beat the apples, gradually adding the sugar. Beat egg whites separately. When the apples have cooled, incorporate egg whites into the apples. Cover a baking sheet with baking paper and pour the mixture at a thickness of 1-2 cm (0.4-0.8 inches). Dry the mixture in the oven, starting at 60-70°C (140-158°F) and then lowering the temperature to 40-50°C (104-122°F). Keep drying it until it can be taken off the baking paper and rolled up (the mixture will thin out and become dark during the drying). Wrap the rolled pastille in cellophane and store it in the refrigerator. Cut it into slices to serve. You can also use it to decorate cakes and tortes.

133

REFRESHING BEVERAGES

"Warmbeer"

This is a highly traditional Latvian beverage and one which has been made on farms where both fresh milk and home-brewed beer are available. In the Vidzeme region of Latvia, farm women would boil fresh milk and add home-brewed beer, stirring the mixture and drinking it on the spot — three measures of milk to one measure of beer, depending on the bitterness of the beer. When milk and beer are mixed together, they have to be stirred vigorously to keep the milk smooth. The beverage was popular in place of tea or coffee at breakfast. On the Kurzeme farms, women would add eggs and sugar to the beverage, making it more appealing to guests.

Ashberry brew

1 l (1 quart + 4 tablespoons) water,
150 g (5.25 oz) ashberries,
80-100 g (3.5 oz) sugar

Pick ripe berries for this drink. Rinse them and then mash them up. Pour water over the berries. Bring to a boil and set aside for 2-3 hours. Strain the liquid and add sugar. Bring the liquid to a boil one more time. Allow to cool before serving.

Cranberry drink

150 g (5.25 oz) cranberries,
1 l (1 quart + 4 tablespoons) water,
85-100 g (3.5 oz) sugar,
1/8 lemon

Rinse and press up the cranberries to get their juice. Put the pulp in a pot along with the water. Bring to a boil and strain. Add the sugar to the liquid and bring it to a boil. Add the fresh cranberry juice and let cool. Pour the drink into a pitcher and decorate it with slices of lemon. You can use currants, strawberries and raspberries for the same process.

Jasmine drink

1 l (1 quart + 4 tablespoons) water,
1/3 teaspoon lemon juice,
40 jasmine blossoms,
4 tablespoons honey

Boil the water and lemon juice. Let the water cool and pour it over the jasmine blossoms. Cover the pot and set it aside for several hours. Strain the liquid. Add the honey. Stir until the honey has melted. Refrigerate thoroughly before serving. You may use dandelion blossoms for this drink, too.

Mint drink

1 l (1 quart + 4 tablespoons) water,
1/3 teaspoon lemon juice,
1-2 tablespoons sugar,
2 tablespoons dried mint,
ice

Boil the water with the lemon juice and sugar. When the liquid has reached boiling, drop the mint into the liquid. Cover the pot and let it cool. Strain. Add lemon juice and sugar to taste to the liquid. Serve iced.

Rye bread drink

1 1/2 l (approximately 1 1/2 quarts) water,
200-250 g (8.75 oz) rye bread or 100-150 g
*   (3.5-5.25 oz) (5.25 oz) rye bread crackers,*
75 g (2.625 oz) sugar,
lemon juice,
ice

Thinly slice the rye bread and put it in a warm oven to dry out (skip this step if you're using crackers). Put the bread in a dish. Pour 1 l (1 quart + 4 tablespoons) of boiling water over it. Cover the dish and set aside for 3-4 hours. When the liquid is brown and tastes and smells like rye bread, strain it. Pour another 1/2 liters of boiling water over the bread. Let it settle for 30-45 minutes, and then strain. Mix together the two liquids and add sugar and lemon juice to taste. Bring to a boil and then allow to cool completely before serving. You may want to add lemon or quince syrup or cranberry or red currant juice to the drink.

Black currant lemonade

150 g (5.25 oz) black currant leaves,
1 1/2 kg (3 lb, 6 oz) sugar,
3/4 glass quince juice,
10 l (10 quarts + 3 cups) water,
50 g (1.75 oz) yeast

Rinse the leaves and put them in a large bowl. Add the sugar and quince juice to the leaves. Bring the water to a boil and add to the bowl as well. Cover the bowl with a cloth and set it aside in a warm place for 24 hours. Crumble the yeast, add it to the mixture and pour it into a container with a tight-fitting lid. Let the mixture ferment for 6 hours. When it is fermented, pour it into bottles and seal tightly. The lemonade will be ready in five days.

Chicory drink

25 g (0.875 oz) ground chicory,
250 g (8.75 oz) apple juice,
750 g (26.25 oz) water,
75 g (2.625 oz) sugar,
ice cubes

Bring 600 g (21 oz) of the water to a boil. Add ground chicory and simmer over a low flame for 3-5 minutes. Strain, reserving the liquid. Boil the remaining water with the sugar. Add the chicory liquid and let the drink cool. Before serving, add the apple juice and mix well. Serve iced.

Kultenis

> *1 kg (2 lb, 3 oz) coarse rye flour,*
> *12-15 l water, 25-50 (0.875-1.75 oz) sugar,*
> *25 g (0.875 oz) yeast,*
> *1/2 l (approximately 1/2 quart) buttermilk*

This is a recipe from Northern Vidzeme. Heat 2 liters of the water to a temperature of 90°C (194°F), and then pour it over the flour. Stir to get a liquid dough. Beat the dough until it becomes light and foamy. Boil the remaining water. Add it to the dough and allow the mixture to cool to 20-25°C (68-77°F). Mix the buttermilk, sugar and yeast (dissolve it in some water first) and add them to the dough. Put the liquid dough in a container (preferably an oak barrel with a tap!). Let the mixture set in a warm place (18-20°C, or 64-68°F) for 10-12 hours. When the liquid dough has risen, put it in the refrigerator until a clear liquid is visible at the top and the flour settles to the bottom. Traditionally the liquid is served as a refreshing beverage for hard working field workers. You can reuse part of the flour at the bottom of the container, adding another flour and water mixture to it. Let the liquid rise for only 4-6 hours. This can be repeated two or three times, but after that start the process anew.

Quince lemonade

> *1 l (1 quart + 4 tablespoons) water,*
> *100 g (3.5 oz) quince,*
> *75-100 g (3.5 oz) sugar, 1/2 glass pine needles*

Thinly slice the quince. Pour the water over the fruit, add the pine needles (rinse them first), and bring the liquid to a boil. Set it aside for 2-3 hours and then strain it. Add the sugar to the liquid, bring it to a boil again, and then allow to cool completely before serving.

Beet drink

> *2 l water, 1 kg (2 lb, 3 oz) beets*

Peel the beets and slice them thinly. Put them in a jar. Boil and then cool the water separately and pour it over the beets. Cover the jar with cheesecloth and let the liquid sour in a warm place (it will develop foam when it has soured). Store the drink in the refrigerator. Beet drink is often mixed with carrot juice and quince syrup, or with sweetened cold tea.

Rhubarb drink

> *200-250 g (7-8.75 oz) rhubarb,*
> *1 l (1 quart + 4 tablespoons) water,*
> *75 g (2.625 oz) sugar,*
> *5-10 g (0.175-0.35 oz) yeast,*
> *10 g (0.35 oz) malt extract or fruit (cranberry or strawberry) juice*

Rinse the rhubarb and slice it into thin rounds. Pour the water over the rhubarb and bring it to a boil. Set aside for 2-3 hours and then strain. Add the sugar, malt extract or berry juice and yeast to the liquid and let it rise for 6-8 hours in a warm place. Let it cool and either serve immediately or fill into bottles. Store the drink in the refrigerator.

Honey brew

250 g (8.75 oz) honey,
1 l (1 quart + 4 tablespoons) water,
the juice of 1/2 lemon or quince juice,
5 g (0.175 oz) yeast

Bring the water to a boil. Add 150 g (5.25 oz) of the honey, stir well and let cool to 20-25°C (68-77°F). Add the lemon or quince juice and the yeast and let rise for 8-10 hours. Add the rest of the honey and let the liquid cool. Pour it into bottles and store in the refrigerator. The drink will be sparkling and tasty in two or three days.

Rye bread brew

1 loaf rye bread,
12.5 l(approximately 13 quarts) water,
1/2 kg (17.5 oz) sugar, 250 g (8.75 oz) honey,
1 jar malt extract syrup,
50 g (1.75 oz) yeast, 1 handful hops

Slice the bread and toast it. Boil 12 liters of the water and pour it over the bread. Set aside for 10 minutes and then drain through a linen napkin. Repeat the procedure twice more. Boil the hops for 15 minutes in 1/2 liter of water and then add the mixture to the rye bread water. Add the honey, syrup and sugar to the mixture while it is still hot, then refrigerate to cool it quickly to a temperature of 20-25°C (68-77°F). Put the yeast in warm water with some sugar to dissolve. Add it to the mixture, and set aside to ferment for 24 hours. (If you ferment it longer, it will turn into alcohol.) Pour into bottles and serve cold.

Holiday drink

10 l (approximately 11 quarts) water,
6 glasses sugar, 4 lemons,
1 handful hops,
2 glasses quince juice,
20 g (0.7 oz) yeast, raisins

Peel and slice the lemons. Put 3 glasses of the sugar in a pan and heat to melt and brown the sugar. Add 2 glasses of sugar to the water and bring it to a boil. Add the quince juice and the melted sugar to the liquid, along with the lemon slices and hops. When the liquid has cooled to 15-20°C (59-68°F), add the yeast, first dissolving it in warm water. Put the beverage in a warm place to ferment overnight. Put 3-5 raisins and a teaspoonful of sugar in a bottle and pour the beverage into the bottle through a sieve to strain it. Repeat with more bottles as needed. Cork the bottles and refrigerate them. The beverage will be ready for drinking in six days.

Sparkling birch juice

Fill fresh birch sap into wine or champagne bottles, adding to each of the bottles 10-15 g (0.35-0.525 oz) sugar, 4-5 raisins and a bit of lemon juice. Do not fill the bottles all the way up. Cork the bottles and put them in a warm place (18-20°C, or 64-68°F) for 4-5 days. Seal the corks thoroughly and store the bottles, lying down, in a cool place (5-10°C, or 41-50°F). The juice will be fermented and sparkling in 15-20 days, and it will have a very pleasant taste indeed.

Pine needle drink

5 glasses water,
2 tablespoons sugar,
200 g (7 oz) pine needles,
1/2 teaspoon lemon juice,
3 tablespoons dried black currant leaves

Rinse green and fresh pine needles in water. Add them gradually to boiling water. Cover the pot and boil for 30 minutes. Strain the liquid and add the sugar, lemon juice and black currant leaves. Cover the pot and let it cool thoroughly. Strain it before serving.

Sorrel drink

1 l (1 quart + 4 tablespoons) water,
100 g (3.5 oz) sorrel,
1-2 tablespoons sugar,
pinch of salt

Chop up the sorrel. Boil the water, add the sorrel, sugar and salt, and cook for 5-8 minutes. Strain the liquid and serve it over ice cubes (add more sugar to taste).

Publisher: Jumava, Dzirnavu iela 73, Riga, LV 1050, Latvia.
Printed in Preses Nams Corp., Jāņa Sēta Printing Group,
Balasta dambis 3, Riga, LV 1081, Latvia.